The Simple Truth

Also by Mary-Alice and Richard Jafolla:

Books

The Quest: A Journey of Spiritual Rediscovery
Adventures on the Quest
The Quest for Prayer
Quest '96
Quest '97
Quest 2000

By Richard Jafolla:

Soul Surgery

Cassette Albums

The Quest: Volumes I and II (abridged audiobook)
Meditations on the Quest

The Simple Truth

Making Sense of God, Life & Other Stuff

Mary-Alice and Richard Jafolla

Unity Books

Fourth edition 2000; tenth printing 2011

To place an order, call the Customer Service Department at 1-800-669-0282, or visit us online at *www.unitybooks.org*.

The publisher wishes to acknowledge the editorial work of Raymond Teague, Michael Maday, and Medini Longwell; the copy services of Tom Lewin, Beth Anderson, and Deborah Dribben; the production help of Rozanne Devine and Jane Blackwood; and the marketing efforts of Allen Liles, Jenee Meyer, and Sharon Sartin.

Cover illustration and design by Karen Rizzo

The New Revised Standard Version was used for all Bible verses, unless otherwise stated.

Library of Congress Cataloging-in-Publication Data

Jafolla, Mary-Alice.

The simple truth: making sense of God, life & other stuff / Mary-Alice and Richard Jafolla.

p. cm.

ISBN 0-87159-247-9 (pbk. : alk. paper)

978-0-87159-247-7

1. Unity School of Christianity—Doctrines. I. Jafolla, Richard. II. Title.

BX9890.U505J33 1999

230'.997—dc21 99-33110

CIP

Canada BN13252 9033 RT

Table of Contents

Beginnings

Hi, Friend—

Ever wonder about yourself—who you are; how others perceive you; and your relationship to other people, to the universe, to God? (And who or what *is* God anyway?) Where do you fit into it all? What is your role? How do you deal with what's going on around you? And then the one we all ask: "Why am I here?"

It's natural to ask these questions, to dig around for explanations, and from time to time to give a bit of heavy-duty thought to them. But can any of us ever *really* come up with the definitive answers to issues of such magnitude? We personally believe as Brian Greene, world-renowned string-theory physicist, does. He describes an "aha" moment he experienced as a teenager while riding a subway: "I was feeling that way that adolescents sometimes get. You know—'What does it all mean? What is life all about?' The usual questions. And I remember thinking, 'Well, people have thought about these issues for ages, and it's not likely that I'm going to have any answers.' But it did occur to me that if I was able to get a thorough familiarity of what the questions *actually were* . . . I would get a certain kind of satisfaction" (*New York*, Feb. 1, 1999, p. 36).

And that's the purpose of this book—to look at some of what *is* known so we can have the satisfaction of being familiar with what the real questions are. This in itself is a noble pursuit. Sometimes we try to look for complicated reasons and hidden meanings, believing that if something is of great importance it has to be difficult to understand. Not necessarily true. To once again quote Brian Greene from the magazine, "At rock bottom, there is a coherence, a simplicity, an explanatory core to the universe."

This completely revised edition of *The Simple Truth* is intended to bring a little light to some of the more important questions and help you start putting wheels on what you know. We see the book as a bridge between spiritual ideals and the reality of your present life. To help you commute from one to the other, we've constructed each chapter in two parts—***The Wisdom*** and ***The Wheels.***

The Wisdom

The first half of each chapter, ***The Wisdom***, presents a basic universal principle. This is background material for you to read and digest so that, like the food you eat, it literally becomes part of you.

While no one would presume any of us are actually living the ideal, completely enlightened life—a life that perfectly mirrors every spiritual principle presented here—at least we can know what we are aiming for.

Once Over Lightly wraps up every ***Wisdom*** section, listing the key points of the chapter. Understanding is a necessary step that comes before doing, so read each ***Wisdom*** section before moving on to ***The Wheels.***

The Wheels

There are two ways to get to the top of an oak tree—climb the tree or sit on an acorn and wait.

The second half of each chapter, ***The Wheels,*** breathes life into the principle. It helps you climb the oak tree. After all, what good is knowing something if you don't put it to use in your life? Each ***Wheels*** contains a:

- **Ponder Point** section designed to get you to examine the principle from different perspectives. Something for you to chew on!
- **Warm-Ups** section to help you to "own" the principle and lead you into some simple real-life action.
- **Going for It** section, a little something to make you stretch, mentally and spiritually.

Wheels is exactly what the name says—it's setting the universal truths into motion in your life and your world. Getting things rolling, so to speak.

You'll notice each *Wheels* section begins with a lighthearted quotation. These are reminders that life is meant to be fun, seasoned generously with smiles and laughter, even when—or maybe *especially* when—we're dealing with the profound!

We hope you enjoy the book and find it helpful. As you journey through its pages, you may discover that your questions and issues are not as complex as you'd imagined and that underlying everything is a very . . . *Simple Truth!*

Our blessings to you,

Mary-Alice and Richard Jafolla

Chapter 1

What Is God?

The Wisdom

How important is
it to define God?

A man spent years searching for the definition of God. He traveled to every continent, meeting with great sages and religious leaders and studying ancient wisdoms. Still no definition. Finally, when almost broke, he heard about a certain guru living in the mountains of Nepal who could define God. The man hired a Sherpa guide and climbed for days, camping out in terrible wind and rainstorms. At last he made it to the top of the mountain and there, sitting on a ledge, was the guru.

"Oh, guru," the man pleaded, "I've traveled thousands of miles and spent all of my money to find the definition of God. Tell me, please, what it is."

The guru stroked his beard, looked up at the sky,

and after many moments of silence said, "God is a fountain."

"God is a fountain?" replied the exasperated man. "That's it? After all this time and money, that's what you tell me, that God is a fountain?"

The guru looked puzzled. "You mean God is *not* a fountain?"

Who are *we* to tell *you* what God is?

When it comes to trying to define God, we all run smack into a wall of impossibility because defining something limits it. If we can define something, it usually means we see its boundaries, its beginning and end. It's implying we know pretty much all there is to know about the subject. Since God is all there is to know, how could we possibly comprehend that! Still, while we aren't able to know and understand *all* of what God is, we can at least know and understand *some* of what God is. We can glimpse very small bits of what we call God. We can know *some*thing of God because we know something of ourselves, our friends, our towns, our families, our pets. And maybe that's enough.

Totally God

Nevertheless, there are some characteristics of God that are worth knowing about. One is location. *Where* is God?

All you see, from the book in front of you to the farthest star, is part of God. You are part of God, and so is everyone on Earth. In fact, Earth itself is part of God. Even the things we cannot see, such as sounds, smells, and feelings, are part of God. To put it succinctly, *everything* is part of God.

So, obviously, there is no place, from the tiniest cell of your body to the largest galaxy in the universe, where God is not. All people and all things are part of the *one* thing we call God. This makes us, literally, all related to each other since we all have the same "parent." (Although God is sometimes referred to as Father, God is clearly not a person.)

The concept of God is so vast, and there is so much about life we don't yet know. Yet we do know God is not separate from creation, and that God is everything. E-V-E-R-Y-T-H-I-N-G!

Mind to the Max

Also, God *knows* everything. God *is* all knowledge. Since we are part of God, our minds are part of God's mind. In other words, there is one God Mind, and everyone's mind is part of it. This is truly a critical concept because it holds that we can receive wonderful ideas and answers from God's mind if we look for them. Imagine getting ideas from God firsthand! Talk about being plugged into the Source! (More of this later.)

It gets even better. The perfect intelligence of God is not only in our brains, it's within every cell of our bodies. God's intelligence directs all of the marvelous tasks of each cell so the entire body can function. Each cell knows exactly what to do and how to do it. The God-power within you knows how to take the nourishing food you eat and turn it into strong, healthy body tissues. It knows how to make your heart beat and your lungs breathe. It does these incredible things without your awareness of them.

Atom-Smashing Power

Okay, so God is everything and everywhere, and God is also all of the knowledge and ideas that ever existed or ever will exist in the future. In fact, we can say God is really a Mind, and because God is everywhere, this Mind—this Supreme Intelligence—is everywhere as well.

And there's *still* more. In addition to being everywhere present *(omnipresent)* and all-knowing *(omniscient)*, God is also all-powerful *(omnipotent)*. There is not a single thing you can think of that is too difficult for God to do. *Nothing* is impossible for God. Couple this with the certainty that the Creator loves what It creates (why else would It create?), and you have a force that impels us toward what's best for each of us and the entire world. Although at times we may not think this is so, let's remember we see only a minuscule fragment of the picture. We can easily overlook a blessing staring us in the face, and we often do.

"Wait! Hold it right there."

"Don't give me this God-is-good stuff. A classmate shot my best friend while she was sitting right at her desk. My mother's being treated for depression, and my brother is in a drug rehab facility. I'm scared most of the time, and I don't even know whom to trust anymore or what's real. I look around and I don't see much evidence of God."

You're right, friend. We live in unsettling times. There's danger and pain and anger all around us. The news media feed on the stuff and we're all touched by it in one way or another. Let's get real—no one can say these things do not exist or that they don't affect us, because they do.

But the ***Wisdom*** offered in this book can be solid support to help you deal with whatever you're dealing with. All the principles presented are time-tested and true. While we may not be at a point where we can rise above or avoid all that's going on around us, we can improve the comfort level of our lives by understanding and then using—***putting wheels on***—some of these principles.

The world gets into trouble when people forget

they are part of God. They try to do things their way, which blocks the mighty flow of God's power. Examples of this phenomenal power of God? How about holding the planets in their orbits around the sun? How about making the tides of the ocean rise and fall? How about pushing the flowers out of the ground each spring? And then there's this one—it is God's power that gives you life and awareness.

The REAL Answer

While it's fine to try to define God, the bottom line is this: We simply cannot do it. But that's okay because ultimately a definition may not be important anyway. Knowing *about* something is not the same as *knowing* something. What we are searching for, after all, is not so much explanation as experience. We want to *feel* the presence of God. That is our goal. As we progress together through these chapters, may we each come to sense the Sacred Presence at work in our lives.

Once Over Lightly–

- You cannot possibly comprehend all that God is, since God *is* all.
- You can know tiny bits of what God is.
- God is everywhere.
- God is all knowledge.
- God is all power.

- The world gets into trouble when people forget they are part of God.
- What we are searching for is not so much explanation as it is experience. We want to *feel* the presence of God.

The Wheels

"If God lived on Earth, people would break his windows."

—Yiddish proverb

Strange that electricity, so universally used, is not really understood. Yet we can gain some understanding of it by observing electricity at work and seeing its effects. We define it, not by what it is—we don't know what it is—but by what it does.

Like love. Can we really define love? Philosophers and poets have been trying for thousands of years, but some things simply do not lend themselves to being identified or defined. Love is one of those things. No one can define it, but we all know love when we experience it. So what does it matter if we can't *define* love? We can still know it and feel it in our own lives. That's what counts.

Same with God. How could we ever define God—how could we define something that is all there is? We can't. But we can experience God—not the totality of God to be sure, but we can have an individual experience of God just as we can have an individual experience of the wind without being tossed around by every wind that ever blew.

Maybe we should stop trying to define the indefinable. Maybe we should stop trying to understand God and simply *experience* God. Just as a kite gives itself fully to the wind, never asking for an explanation or a definition of what the wind is, let's dare to give ourselves fully to God and allow God to take us to the very heights of our spiritual potential.

Ponder Point

Can you imagine if each time your heart were supposed to beat, *you* had to remind it to do so? Or each time your lungs needed air, you had to tell them to inhale? Unthinkable. Impossible. Have you ever really considered all the fantastic mechanical, chemical, and electrical processes that go on in your body without needing your direction?

No scientific genius in the world can do the amazing things that one single cell of your body can do. Spend a few minutes each day—before nodding off at night works well—reflecting on how ingeniously and how intelligently you are made. Try to realize what kind of mind God must have to be able to create something as wonderful as a human being!

Warm-Ups

1. *Begin today to look for signs of God.* Look for God in people and in things. Sense God's masterful intelligence at work, making plants and trees grow, and making your body function as it does. Feel God's supreme power in the wind, in the turning of Earth from day to night, and in the little weed that pushes up through the cracks in the concrete of a wall or sidewalk.

No matter what's going on around you, see how many ways and in how many places you can find evidence of God. (HINT: The more you look, the more you will find.) As you discover evidence of God, take a second to realize how incredibly fortunate you are to be part of this Creator who can produce such miracles.

2. *Cite an obvious evidence of God in your life:*

Going for It

God is, hands down, the superstar of the Bible. Yet in all of its hundreds of pages, the Bible offers us only one definition of God (1 Jn.4:8). The definition? "God is love." *What are your thoughts about this being the only definition?*

Chapter 2

The Awesome Threesome

The Wisdom

What we see and hear in the outer world can be unreliable.

Spirit, soul, and body. We hear the words, but what do they mean? *Spirit* and *soul* seem especially confusing, although they are two very different concepts, as we'll soon see. We need to get a handle on Spirit, soul, and body so we can understand the roles they play in our lives. Serving *them* better helps them serve *us* better.

We're asking you to please hang in here while we cover the information in this chapter. It may not be glamorous or exciting, but it's info we need if we want to feel in charge of our lives instead of feeling like helpless victims. (Actually, this info has the potential to become *very* exciting once you catch the impact of what it holds for you.) Okay. On with the "awesome threesome."

Spirit—The Invincible You

Your *Spirit* is changeless. It's the "real" you—the aspect of you that recognizes your divinity, recognizes that God lives *as you*. You will always want to feel connected with your Spirit, because it will unerringly guide you in ways that are best for you.

When you are able to sense the presence of God—in yourself and in everyone else—you will be living from your spiritual dimension. Not there yet? Join the club. Yet the surprising thing is that right now on some level deep within you, your Spirit does love everyone and everything because everyone and everything are part of God, part of you. All people have the same divinity as you do, no matter how it may appear otherwise at times.

Soul—The Changeable You

Another aspect of you is your soul. Constantly changing, it is made up of your thoughts and feelings and everything else in your mind. Your soul *is* your mind—your personality. It decides the way you act. It decides how you feel and how you express your feelings. It decides what you say. Although it can't be seen or heard or touched, it nevertheless determines how your life unfolds and makes you what you are.

Think of your soul as a swinging door. It can open in or out. If it opens inwardly—in other words, if we turn to the spiritual aspect of us—we will receive all the marvelous ideas we need in order to be happier and to live more satisfying lives. When we do this, we say we are turning our souls inward to Spirit, or God.

The soul can also turn to the outer world, influenced by all the things and people and events around us. When the soul focuses on these things, it often receives false information. Something can seem "bad" or sadden us because we're judging with only our five senses. Since what we see and hear in the outer world is often unreliable, it's best to make it a habit to turn to that God Self inside us for correct promptings on what to say or what to do in every situation.

There's one great reason why the soul should be filled with correct info: *Your life will reflect what is in your soul!* Let's look at what this means. Whatever you really believe, feel strongly about, and think about constantly will tend to show up in your life. You see, the soul is like a factory. It doesn't care *what* it produces—it just produces. But it can only produce what it has been told to produce. Like a reliable building contractor, your soul follows the blueprint of your thoughts and feelings.

For instance, if an intelligent child has been consistently told he is not smart and if deep in his soul he has accepted this as a "fact," he will find a way to get poor grades. And he will continue to do so until his belief changes. Or, if a person *truly* believes she will inherit an illness, the soul will see to it that she does.

Body—The Tangible You

Your *body* is a vehicle through which God is expressed. It's also the home of your soul. People all over the world build beautiful churches, temples, and cathedrals, which they admire and respect as "God's houses." They lavish a lot of time and money preserving and beautifying them. Yet they often forget that first and foremost God dwells within the human body. While no one would consider throwing garbage and trash into one of these man-made houses of God, many throw "garbage and trash" into their bodies! When we eat and drink harmful foods and beverages or use harmful substances, we do just that—we damage the temple that God constructed. We also damage the body when we hold onto hate-filled thoughts and other negative thoughts. Since the body is a temple for God, shouldn't it be cared for and respected?

Recapping

Spirit, soul, and body are key concepts, so let's quickly review them. Spirit is your essence and your awareness of God living through you, giving you access to the gifts and attributes of God.

Your soul comprises your thoughts, beliefs, attitudes, and feelings about things. The soul can "tune in" to your Spirit or it can "tune in" to the world. The choice you make affects your entire life, so it needs to be as Spirit-centered and loving as you can make it.

Your body is the home of God. It deserves to be treated accordingly.

Once Over Lightly–

- You have three aspects—Spirit, soul, and body.
- Your Spirit is the unchanging, divine aspect of you.
- Your soul is your mind and emotions—the changeable you.
- Your body is a vehicle through which God is expressed.

The Wheels

"It's so important to know you can choose to feel good. Most people don't think they have that choice."

—Neil Simon

Our object is to express our unique God Self. In order to attempt this, there needs to be a constant source of inspiration available to us, a "well" we can draw from, a pattern we can copy. Spirit is the ultimate inspiration, the infinite well, the perfect pattern. This is why identifying with the spiritual aspect of ourselves is crucial. Spirit is the eternal, unchanging nucleus of us, the absolute essence of what we are. And from this Spirit, from this well, flow the ideas of the mind of God. The flow never dries up since the Source is infinite. But the hitch is that we can utilize only as much as our souls are capable of accepting. After all, a well may tap into unlimited gallons of water, but if we bring only a small glass to fill, that's all the water we'll be able to get.

The soul is like the container we bring to the well. That's why the role of the soul is critical. Spirit makes available infinite inspiration, but we can bring into our lives only the amount that our souls can contain. So why not bring a bucket!

Ponder Point

Try this on for size: *You always were and you always will be.* It's true. The essence of you, your Spirit—the "you" that is integral to completing God's universe—was never born and will never die. How could it, when it's part of an ageless, eternal, infinite God—a God that just won't quit?

Warm-Ups

The soul is the sum total of all we are willing to accept from the Spirit. It is pivotal in that it not only touches the Spirit where it receives inspiration but also touches the external world where it receives impressions. The soul makes a choice: Do I look inside myself for inspiration and guidance or do I look to the world?

1. *A specific example from my life of when I looked inward for guidance and wisdom:*

2. *A specific example from my life of when I looked to the world for guidance and wisdom:*

Going for It

We've said the soul can receive pure inspiration from God through our Spirit or it can receive faulty impressions from the outer world through our limited five senses. Depending on which direction the soul takes, our lives are either God-directed or world-directed. Now consider this: If Spirit could somehow bypass the soul to inspire and motivate the body directly, the body would have to be perfect. Ahhh . . . but there would be a humongous price to pay. We would have lost one of the greatest gifts God has given us: our freedom of choice. Without free will we would be automatons, marionettes on a string. But we are obviously *not* mere marionettes, because we have free will—the ability to accept or reject our spirituality and all the blessings it can bring us.

What are your thoughts about free will?

Chapter 3

All Aboard! Everyone Needed

The Wisdom

There's a cosmic project going on, and we're all invited.

Diogenes, the Greek philosopher who died circa 323 B.C.E., was known for his unconventional ways of teaching. One day Alexander the Great was surprised to come upon Diogenes examining a pile of human bones. "What are you looking for?" he asked.

"I am searching for the bones of your father," Diogenes replied, "but I cannot distinguish them from those of his slaves."

We already know God lives through every person absolutely equally. So it obviously doesn't matter what skin or hair color people have; what church, temple, or mosque they worship in; where they work or live; or what language they speak. Every human being is created by God and is a means through which God expresses life and works out the universal plan. This is major information. When enough people know God is in *all* people, wars and crimes and hatefulness in the world will make their exit. In fact, here's a foolproof equation—the amount of love and peace we have in the world at any given time is directly proportionate to the degree that we all recognize God in each other.

Laws and governments can't legislate peace. That's as obvious today as it has been for five thousand years. It can only happen when each person knows that God is within *all* people, not just himself or herself, family, and friends. Perhaps this sounds too much to hope for, yet you, personally, can add to the peace in the world by becoming more aware of God's presence in yourself and others and acting accordingly. Eventually people around you will begin to "get it" too, and the cheer and kindness you kicked off will begin to spread.

Ever toss a stone into a pond and notice the ripples it makes? The rings go out, out, and out. So much action from one small stone at the center! This is a way you can actually help change the world and make it a better place. There you'll be, like the little stone at the center, your kind thoughts and actions rippling out in ever-increasing circles as more and more people begin noticing the changes happening. These changes may be subtle, but they'll be beautiful, and people *will* sense something just got better in their world. Sooner or later others will make their own ripples, and the circles will grow even wider.

Once Over Lightly–

- Every human being is created by God and is a means through which God expresses life and works out the universal plan.
- You can add to world peace by being more aware of God's presence in yourself and others and acting accordingly.
- Eventually the cheer and kindness you kick off will begin to spread as others get in on it.

The Wheels

"There is no they, only us."

—Bumper sticker

What's the use of knowing something can help us if we don't use it to make our lives better? The best part about *knowing* that we are all created equal—that we are all brothers and sisters—is that we automatically treat everyone as an equal. Acknowledging others as equals, we simply can't help treating them with love and respect. The bonus for us is that we are treated with love and respect in return. (Hmmmm . . . ever hear the expression that what goes around comes around?)

Now, of course, all this is the way things are *supposed* to be. But rather than freaking out over not even coming close, we can begin today to make the commitment to doing our own little parts. It's the only way to get from "here" to "there." After all, we *are* all in this together. The ember that falls away from the fire becomes cold, because it has separated from its family.

Ponder Point

Imagine if—in *every* situation, in *every* interaction, with *every* person—you consistently acted with love and respect. Now think of all the daily interactions you have: face-to-face, over the telephone, by e-mail. Multiply that by 365 days each year. That's hundreds of thousands, perhaps millions, of interactions you will have in a lifetime. Like a bee pollinating each flower it touches, how can you not affect the world in a positive way! And it all begins with the assurance in your own heart that everyone on Earth is equally a child of the one Creator—God.

What can you do **right now** *to turn your wheels in this direction?*

Warm-Ups

1. *Comment on a time in the past (or perhaps the present!) when you felt you were either better or worse than another person. This could be a feeling based on intelligence or physical looks or popularity or anything else.*

2. Considering the **Wisdom** *of this chapter, analyze your comments to #1. Did (or does) your reasoning seem strong or shallow? In what way?*

Going for It

The fact that we are all created equal and are all equally part of God should really be the most basic foundation for any relationship. Yet discrimination based on color of skin, religious belief, and nationality generates more hatred than perhaps any other reason. People who believe in the inequality of the human family cannot possibly believe we are all part of God.

Your comments on this:

Chapter 4

How Do I Find God?

The Wisdom

Discovering God is virtually goof-proof.

What do you do when someone gives you a present? Rip it open to see what's inside, right? But what if you took that present, stuck it on a shelf unopened, and let it sit for months or even years? Technically, you've been given a gift. But what good is it if you don't take off the wrapping and discover what's inside?

God is a gift waiting to be discovered, and making the discovery is virtually goof-proof. No matter how you go about it, you can't go wrong in finding God—you *are* going to succeed. All you need is the strong desire to become aware of God. Until you do, there's always that antsy feeling that things are not going as well as they could for you—that something is missing. If this describes *you*, open the gift.

Open the gift by thinking about God. Look for evidence of God all around you. Find God in the smile of a stranger in a shopping mall, for instance. Find God in the fragile newborn leaf on a springtime tree. It's God you see in the playfulness of a puppy. It's God you perceive in the eyes of a longtime friend. It's God you feel in your heart when you love someone. God is in every cell of your body, bringing you life. And that "inner voice" telling you the right thing to say or do? You got it—God again.

There's *no* place where you cannot find God if you really look. Okay, so there are times when you have to look extremely hard, but don't give up. Keep on looking—God *is* there! Most important, keep reminding yourself that God is *within you.*

Your mind is your link with God. With your mind you *think* about God, and you *feel* God's love and power. So the quickest way to find God is by using your mind to look inside yourself.

Anyone who searches for God will succeed. God is never lost, nor does God play hide-and-seek with us. God hasn't gone anywhere. The sacred presence of our Creator always has been and always will be . . . ***everywhere***, and it is most intimately experienced right inside ourselves. This sweet presence is God's megagift to us. We just have to unwrap it.

Once Over Lightly–

- God is a gift waiting to be discovered.
- No matter how you go about it, you can't go wrong in finding God—you're going to succeed.
- There's no place you cannot find God if you really look.
- The quickest way to find God is by using your mind to look inside yourself.

The Wheels

"Live in such a way that you would not be ashamed to sell your parrot to the town gossip."

—Will Rogers

A popular song some years back dealt with looking for love in all the wrong places. It was easy to identify with the lyrics because many of us have looked for love in people and in circumstances that were simply dead ends.

It could be that some of us have also been looking for God in all the wrong places. We've looked for God in churches, synagogues, and mosques. We've searched in sweat lodges, monasteries, and mountaintops. Thinking they would lead us to God, we've joined this group and that group and followed gurus, rabbis, preachers, and teachers. We've looked everywhere but in our own hearts.

The simple truth is we don't have to go anywhere or follow anyone to find God, just as we don't have to go anywhere or follow anyone to find ourselves. God and we are one!

Ponder Point

Does saying "God and I are one" mean that we are God?

If a drop of ocean water said "The ocean and I are one," would you think the drop thought it was the ocean? It's easy to understand that the drop of ocean water and the ocean are inseparable. On one hand, it's also easy to understand that the drop is not the entire ocean. It can be one with the ocean without losing its singular identity and without being the entire ocean. In the same way, knowing that God and we are one doesn't mean we are the totality of God.

On the other hand, if the drop is in the ocean,

can it truly be said that it is in any way distinct from the ocean?

Warm-Ups

Be on the lookout for sightings of God. We get so carried away with our own "stuff" that we forget to recognize the presence of God in the midst of things. We forget that help is on the way. In fact, it's already arrived.

1. *Can you describe a situation when you suddenly were aware there was a Higher Power at work?*

2. *Can you describe a situation when you believed God was* not *present? How would things have been different if they had played out with your believing God* was *present?*

Going for It

Put a hold on reality for a minute and imagine a drop of water in the ocean as having reasoning power. This little drop is on a quest to find the ocean. Now imagine yourself going on a quest to find God. *What are the similarities?*

Chapter 5

Gifts Galore

The Wisdom

Access your 24-hour-a-day inheritance.

"I am a child of God." People often refer to themselves this way, or they might call God their Father. We probably use these words because it's a simple way to understand our relationship to God.

In a sense God is our Father *and* our Mother as well. God is our Creator and, just as any good parent would, offers us wonderful gifts. These gifts are not money, clothes, or cars—they're much better than those. God gives us minds and fills them with ideas we can use to bless our lives.

These ideas from God are called *spiritual gifts*, and they are our inheritance from God. The more we realize we have these spiritual gifts, the more we will utilize them to create better lives for ourselves. Although they are available 24 hours a day, God's gifts are not always obvious to us. Too much noise, too much excitement and confusion all the time for us to notice. So how do we discover them? By listening to our inner "voice."

A really profound story in the New Testament clearly illustrates how we inherit God's gifts. It's commonly referred to as the story of "The Prodigal Son." Here's the gist of it:

A man had two sons. The younger one, after asking his father to give him his full share of his inheritance, took the money and left home. He soon squandered the entire inheritance on meaningless things, and ended up with no money, even for food.

Remembering how much better things were back at his father's house, he decided to return home. Ashamed and sorry for having been such a jerk, he humbly begged his father to treat him not as a son but as a servant. But the father was so overjoyed to have his son back that he gave him a ring and beautiful clothes, and had a great feast prepared to celebrate the return.

Meanwhile, the older son became jealous of all the attention and gifts being lavished on his brother. He said it wasn't fair—that he'd been a loyal son and hadn't run away as his brother had, and yet he'd never been treated to such gifts and celebrations. But his father explained to him that his thinking was wrong. The father told the older son that he had always been a part of him and that everything he owned had always been his, simply for the asking.

How ironic! The older brother had had access to his father's riches all the time, but obviously never took advantage of them, never asked for them! And this is exactly what *we* do when we aren't aware of God's spiritual gifts, so we never allow them to enrich our lives.

Think of the father and how he loved both his sons and was willing to give them everything he had. This gives you some idea of your relationship to God, who—because of unconditional love for you—has already given you access to everything you need. Sometimes human parents, unwilling or unable to show their love and tenderness, are abusive and cruel to their children. Not so with God, the One who doesn't even have the *ability* to mistreat us or stop loving us. This is our eternal Parent, and the gifts are always waiting for us.

Once Over Lightly–

- God has given you spiritual gifts—ideas you can use to bless your life.
- God has already given you access to everything you need.
- The gifts are always waiting for you.

The Wheels

"You are not really successful until someone claims he sat beside you in school."

—James S. Hewett

Several years ago there was a story in the newspaper of a man who was holding a winning lottery ticket and didn't know it. He had somehow misplaced the ticket and, the week before it was about to expire, discovered it in an old pair of pants. He checked it out and was stunned to learn the incredible news. He was a multimillionaire for almost a year and never knew it. During that entire year he had struggled financially. Constantly behind in car payments, mortgage payments, and credit card payments, he'd had a difficult time just trying to make ends meet. Ironically, he'd had access to fabulous wealth beyond his wildest dreams, but didn't know it.

Ponder Point

One of Ripley's "Believe It or Not" features showed a plain bar of iron with a value of $5. Turn the iron bar into horseshoes, and the value goes up to $50, the item states. Make it into needles, and the worth soars to $5,000. Make it into balance springs for delicate Swiss watches, and that same bar of iron becomes worth $500,000. The moral of the story is that the same raw material can be worthless or priceless. It all depends on how we use it.

That's what this chapter is all about. We are fabulously wealthy, beyond anything we can imagine. But we may not fully know it because our wealth is in the form of ideas—*divine* ideas, which are ours to develop. Like the bar of iron, these ideas can be turned into something mediocre or we can mold them into priceless blessings.

Warm-Ups

Once we know we are part of God and all of God's blessings, we begin to act like children of God. We begin to take advantage of the divine gifts we have inherited. We begin to enjoy the security of forever having access to all that the Father has. What's God's is ours.

Do you listen for the stupendous ideas God has for you? *What specifically can you do to become more aware of your enormous wealth in the form of ideas?*

Going for It

The story of "The Prodigal Son" (Lk. 15:11-32) is a fairly short story. Read it and, as you do, think about the two brothers. Try to feel how each of them felt.

Which one are you most like? (Is it the one who didn't realize how fortunate he was or the other one, who wasted his gifts?)

Which more accurately defines you? In what way(s)?

Chapter 6

Count on It

The Wisdom

Solid gold, diamond-studded, ironclad—God's laws are 100 percent reliable.

Space is curved—Albert Einstein was sure of it. He based the prediction on his general theory of relativity, but couldn't prove it. Then a 1919 expedition to observe the solar eclipse confirmed his prediction—space *is* curved. Later a pupil asked Einstein, "What would you have said if there had been no confirmation of this kind?"

"I would have been obliged to pity our dear God," Einstein said. "The theory is correct."

God has set up the universe so that everything functions according to perfect law. In the overall scheme of things, there exists an eternal movement toward order and harmony and spiritual evolution.

The entire universe functions according to God's laws. The tides rise and fall according to God's law. An oak tree grows from an acorn because of law. The moon orbits Earth and Earth orbits the sun because of law. If you plant tomato seeds, you get tomatoes and not carrots, because seeds grow according to law.

What a relief to know there's one thing in this world we can always count on—*God never breaks promises!* God's "promises" are another way of saying "laws," and God's laws never change. They are solid gold, diamond-studded, ironclad, 100 percent reliable.

Our Part of the Contract

While it's true we can always count on God to keep promises to us, in order for those promises to be fulfilled we have *our* share to do. If we want to enjoy God's blessings to the max, we have to obey God's laws. This means making wise use of our inheritance from God, and doing our best every day to cooperate with God's laws. It begins with thinking positive thoughts, saying uplifting words, and doing kind and loving things. But it also includes eating nourishing foods, exercising on a regular basis, finding quiet times daily. These are some of the ways we can cooperate with the laws God created for us. The fact that God can always be relied upon to respond to our sincere efforts has to be some of the best comfort and reassurance we can ever have.

We'll come back to God's laws in the next chapter. For now, it's enough to understand that God can never break promises. The laws of the universe apply to us all, and we are meant to cooperate with them as best we can. God will not suspend or circumvent any law at any time. You can count on it. Plant those tomato seeds, and you'll get tomatoes. God designed it that way.

Once Over Lightly–

- God has set up the universe so that everything functions according to perfect law.
- God's laws never change. You can always count on them.
- If you want to enjoy God's blessings to the max, you have to obey God's laws.

The Wheels

"The scientific theory I like best is that the rings of Saturn are composed entirely of lost airline luggage."

—Mark Russell

We're talking God's laws here. Man-made laws are a whole other story. One city may pass a law banning handguns while another says they are legal to own. One state has a speed limit of 70 miles per hour while another says it's against the law to do more than 65. Some man-made laws are so hard to interpret that they go all the way to the Supreme Court for a final verdict. And fifty years later members of another Supreme Court may overturn the opinion of their predecessors.

God's laws, on the other hand, are immutable. Once discovered, they can be counted on to be consistent.

Mostly we are familiar with God's laws having to do with the sciences. We rely on the law of gravity to keep us from spinning off into space. We know the laws of aerodynamics that allow us to design vehicles which fly. We know at sea level water will boil at 212 degrees Fahrenheit. Knowing that the laws will hold true for all places and at all times allows us to plan our lives with as few surprises and dangers as possible.

But God's laws are not only those physical laws that have been discovered. There are also mental laws, such as this: *Thoughts held in mind produce after their kind* (more of this later in the book), and there are even spiritual laws like the Golden Rule and the laws of love and forgiveness. All of these laws are as changeless as any physical laws, and can be relied on just as absolutely.

Ponder Point

In Chapter 1 you were asked to consider all of the fantastic processes that go on in your body without needing your conscious direction. For instance, what would happen if you had to remember to tell your heart to beat or your lungs to take in air? In the same vein, consider for a moment what would happen if God's laws were not universal or consistent. What if your body suddenly decided it didn't need oxygen but helium? What if gravity worked only on Mondays, Wednesdays, and Fridays? What if ships floated only some of the time? How about airplanes—what if the laws of aerodynamics were suddenly suspended because God got tired of them?

Warm-Ups

There may be a tendency to think that mental laws are higher laws than physical laws and that spiritual laws are higher than both, but this is not true. It couldn't be true because then we could use mental laws and spiritual laws to change physical laws. We could somehow will an airplane to stop flying or use our mental or spiritual powers to jump off a building and glide down to a safe landing.

You may be thinking that Jesus used "higher" laws to walk on water or heal the sick. But he didn't use higher laws; he used *other* laws. There are no higher or lower laws; there are only God's laws. Obviously, Jesus used laws we have not discovered yet. For instance, although the laws of flight were in existence during Jesus' time, they hadn't been discovered yet, so if a helicopter were to have somehow flown over Jerusalem two thousand years ago, everyone would have thought it was a miracle or some airborne monster. The laws existed, but simply were undiscovered.

What does this do to the idea of miracles? Can there be such a thing as a miracle?

Going for It

In the early 1900s many people were in favor of closing the United States Patent Office to save money, because they thought all of the scientific discoveries had been made and therefore any further inventions were unlikely. In fact in 1899, Charles H. Duell, the U.S. commissioner of patents, announced, "Everything that can be invented has been invented." Since that time, of course, there have been hundreds of thousands of inventions that have radically changed the way we live.

What about God's laws, other than the physical discoveries we have made? The Bible talks about ten laws that we call the Ten Commandments. These commandments do not specifically deal with love or forgiveness or compassion. *What laws not mentioned in the Ten Commandments do you see as important in your life?*

Chapter 7

The Granddaddy of All Laws

The Wisdom

Tomato seeds don't grow apples.

- A basketball swishes through the hoop [effect] because it was shot accurately [cause].
- It was shot accurately [effect] because the player practiced every day [cause].
- The player practiced every day [effect] because he wanted to be a great basketball player [cause].

Cause and effect means that for every result or thing that exists—an *effect*—there is something that made it happen—a *cause*. Every single occurrence happens (and is happening) as a result of a specific cause. Although we speak about the *laws* of God as if there were many, they all follow the law of cause and effect.

When you exercise regularly, your body grows stronger. Proper exercise is the cause, increased strength, more energy, and better body proportions, the effect. On the other hand, what about the perpetual couch potato? The effect of never exercising is obvious—weakened muscles, lack of energy, and a body that will more and more resemble a spud!

SPECIAL NOTE: While the law of cause and effect is *always* operative, the effect may not always follow the cause as obviously as the above examples because we don't necessarily reap *where* we sow. Roughly interpreted, this means if a thief steals from someone, he might not have someone steal from *him*. But the law always does balance things, and so unless the thief changes his ways, he can expect to reap a negative effect at some point in his life.

While waiting for someone in the lobby of a deluxe hotel, a friend of ours observed a man take a wad of gum he was chewing, stick it on the back of an elegant leather chair, and walk away. Our friend was really incensed by the man's crudeness. Almost immediately, a woman leaned against the chair and the gum stuck to her jacket. When she realized what had happened, she pulled the gum off and dropped it on the floor. It didn't take long for someone to step on it. As soon as he did, he scraped it off his shoe and put it on the back of the same leather chair. At this point, the original gum-chewer returned, saw the gum, and popped it back into his mouth!

What's cool about the law of cause and effect is that we can always count on it to work. The law is actually very simple and in its simplicity lies its elegance. We can expect to receive happiness and blessings in our lives when we set into motion the cause of love and kindness, for instance.

In Chapter 6 we used the example of planting tomato seeds and getting tomatoes, not carrots, because seeds grow according to law. All the miraculous things that take place inside your body operate by the law of cause and effect. Each part knows what to do and how to do it, and when each part does its thing, the effect is predictable. A heart doesn't act like an eye, because it follows the law that made it a heart and tells it what a heart is supposed to do. The cause—its genetic makeup—leads to the effect of a beating heart.

Earth revolves around the sun, and our seasons change according to the law of cause and effect. Everywhere we look we see the workings of God's laws.

The Invisible as Well

But the law of cause and effect does not operate only in the visible world. Everything, including thoughts and feelings and attitudes, is subject to the law. For instance, if you keep a positive and cheerful outlook most of the time, you will tend to have positive and cheerful people and circumstances in your life.

In a nutshell: *Everything, including our thoughts and health and events in our lives, operates according to the law of cause and effect, and this law cannot be broken*. It always works! Every cause we set in motion is eventually but inevitably followed by a corresponding equal effect in our lives. We'll be meeting two other examples of God's laws at work in the chapters on love and prosperity.

Once Over Lightly–

- All God's laws follow the law of cause and effect.
- You don't always reap where you sow.
- Everything in the seen and unseen world operates by the law of cause and effect.
- Every cause you set in motion is eventually but inevitably followed by a corresponding effect in your life.

The Wheels

"Those who go against the grain of God's laws shouldn't complain when they get splinters."

—Unknown

The law of cause and effect can be obvious when dealing with observable phenomena. You throw a bowling ball—it collides with a pin and the pin falls down. Could it be that once in a while a bowling ball will crash into a pin and the pin won't move? Impossible. One of the laws of motion states that for every action there is an *equal* and *opposite* reaction. This is science defining cause and effect. Could it be that this law works only some of the time? Nope. This law works universally, in all cases and in all circumstances in the world of body, mind, and spirit. Live a life of cruelty and hatred, and true joy will never fill your heart. Live a life of cheating, defrauding, and swindling, and what can you really expect?

Ponder Point

When you ponder the implications of it, effect must follow cause in *every* instance. How can an action—any action—take place without a *re*action? Whether or not the reaction is immediate is unimportant. The key point is that it *will* take place. It has to! If just one insignificant example of the law of cause and effect proves to be inconsistent, *all* laws will be inconsistent and the universe, rather than being a cosmos, will be a chaos. The fact that we live in a predictable universe proves the law of cause and effect.

Warm-Ups

Now for the tricky part. It can be difficult for people to apply the law of cause and effect to their own lives. Because the consequences of our actions are often delayed—we don't bother to study math hard enough through elementary school and we have trouble with algebra years later in high school—it's easy to think that our actions will not affect us.

Think of a cause that you put into motion whose effect you are feeling now.

Going for It

Think of some historical facts that show the effect lagging behind the cause by many years. One example would be the unfair taxes the British had been levying on the early colonists which eventuated in the Boston Tea Party. *What other historical examples can you think of?*

Now how about an example from your own life?

Chapter 8

Where's Heaven?

The Wisdom

Take off your space suit;
heaven's not out there.

Take a spaceship to the farthest reaches of the universe, and you'll never find a place called heaven. Why? Because heaven is not a place; it's a state of mind, so . . . *heaven is in you*!

When you accept the fact that you are part of God, and when you live your life as if you really *believe* you are part of God, heaven appears automatically.

Think of it this way: When you do your best to let God be God in you, that's heaven. It was always right here, waiting. You don't have to spend time looking for it. You don't have to go anyplace to find it. All it takes is the realization that wherever you are, God is. And that means, strange as it may sound, you live in heaven right now.

Your awareness that heaven is inside you leads to your awareness that God sees with *your* eyes and hears with *your* ears. God's ideas flow through *your* mind. God uses *your* hands and expresses through *your* body.

When your thoughts and words and actions spring from your higher sense and are the best you can make them . . . that's heaven. When, by opening yourself to Spirit, you turn an angry situation into a peaceful, loving one . . . that's heaven. When, responding from your heart, you take the hand of a friend and let him or her know you care and understand . . . that, too, is heaven.

Heaven can be experienced in limitless ways and places. At any moment of any day you can stop and ask yourself: "Am I remembering I am part of God and everyone else is too? Am I doing my best? Am I *being* my best? Am I seeing God's blessing here? Am I acting with love?" If the answers are "Yes," look around, because you're in heaven.

Once Over Lightly–

- Heaven is not a place; it's a state of mind.
- Heaven is in *you*.
- Heaven can be experienced in limitless ways and places.

The Wheels

"I don't mind going to heaven if I can go to hell every Saturday night."

—Unknown

More of heaven in a minute. First a word about hell. We won't try to define it, just as we did not define heaven. But we all can certainly know what hell feels like. We experience hell when we won't accept the fact that we are part of God and when we insist on living lives which mirror that belief. And so we end up inflicting terrible pressures on ourselves. Adults feel pressured by their jobs, their finances, their spouses, their in-laws, their children. The list is long. Teens feel pressured by grades, competition for college admission, sexual issues, sports, family situations, the mind-set that says: "I *must* excel. I *must* be the best." These stresses can take a huge toll on teenagers, who often look to drugs or even suicide as a way out. For anyone burned out by all the pressures of being a teen or an adult (or even a child), living can be hell.

Ponder Point

If you've been under pressure to achieve, it's time to step back and ask yourself this question: "Am I what I have achieved?" Is what you've achieved (or not achieved) your real identity, or is something else the real you?

Maybe it's time to go back to participating in things simply for the fun of it, without the pressure of having to prove yourself gifted or worthy or competent. Start looking for activities where you can just be yourself, without "making the cut." You'll discover you're not alone in feeling this way. And let us share a secret we, the authors, have learned over the years: The other stuff—the stuff that seems so important, so urgent today—in retrospect, usually turns out to have been no big deal after all.

Warm-Ups

In the *Wisdom* section we suggested asking yourself: *"Am I remembering I am part of God and everyone else is too? Am I doing my best? Am I* being *my best? Am I seeing God's blessing here? Am I acting with love?" If the answers are "Yes," look around, because you're in heaven.*

You can make a game out of asking these questions of yourself throughout the day. But to make it work, you have to be brutally honest. See how many times you catch yourself not being able to answer "Yes." When you do, take immediate steps to change your attitude or actions so that you *can* answer "Yes." NOTE: This is much more difficult than it sounds, because old, negative habits can have a grip on us all like a steel trap. We have to keep breaking loose from them long enough for them to rust away from disuse.

The object of the game, of course, is to catch yourself with more and more "Yes" answers, until finally you *never* have a "No" to any of those questions. Never mind if that seems unattainable. We progress just one day at a time. Work with where you are *today*.

Going for It

If heaven is a state of mind where we feel our connection to God, what do you think hell is?

Chapter 9

Prayer and Meditation

The Wisdom

What a mess it would be if
we could influence God!

"People said they would pray for me. We often take that phrase for granted. I don't take it for granted anymore." These are the heartfelt words of actor Michael J. Fox, whose own life had been touched by prayer after his public announcement that he had Parkinson's disease (*USA Today*, Jan. 25, 1999, p.3D).

What exactly is this mysterious activity called prayer? The Buddhist's spinning a prayer wheel, the Hindu's sitting quietly cross-legged, the Native American's dancing around a fire, the Catholic's lighting a candle, and any of the various other ways people express their desire to feel the presence of God are all legitimate—and effective—forms of prayer.

So let's use this as a working definition: *Prayer is any conscious attempt to experience more of the presence of God.* We can do this by speaking words out loud or silently, or by simply getting quiet. There's not much benefit in repeating a lot of words that are meaningless to us. The important thing in prayer is to really *feel* what we are saying and to believe the experience affects us in a positive way.

Some people think the purpose of prayer is to beg God to give them something or do something to change their lives. But this can't be the purpose of prayer, because we already have access to all that God is. So why bother to pray? Because when we pray—when we sincerely hunger to feel God's presence—something happens to change *us.* When *we* change, we find everything else changes. It's the ultimate makeover!

When we pray and are aware of the presence of God in us, we are resting in what is called the *secret place of the Most High.* "Secret," because no one else has access to it deep within us. And "Most High," because it refers to God. It refers to the place where we make contact with God. No, it's really *more* than that. It's the experience of actually knowing that God is living *as* us! No other experience can even come close.

In prayer, as we sense the presence of God as us, we can indicate our willingness to receive direction for our lives. Spending time in prayer opens our hearts so God can work freely *through* us. This way the right things happen for us.

What's the Catch?

The catch here is that God's way is not always "our" way. God's idea of what is right for us may not be what *we* had in mind. We pray so that God's way will emerge. And if we can let go of our own ideas of how we want things to be, we'll be amazed at the new and wonderful things God has in store for us, far superior to anything *we* had dreamed up.

Wouldn't it be awful if we could influence and bend God to our own wishes and ideas? Every time someone begged for something God would have to change plans. Imagine the chaos of a universe like that! But, fortunately, God never changes. It is we who change. Since God is already completely available to us, it's up to us to recognize this Sacred Presence and allow It to work in our lives.

Our prayers, then, can be those moments when we express our love and appreciation for God. We can express our yearning to feel more of God's presence in ourselves and everywhere else. In other words, we can use our prayer time to experience our Creator. When we do, *we* are transformed.

Getting on God's Wavelength

If prayer in its simplest form is talking to God, then meditation in its simplest form is *listening* to God. Both are important experiences. During meditation we learn to listen for the silent "voice" that comes from deep within us and brings us guidance. This is the voice of God in us, always there to help. We say "voice," but it's usually more like a feeling or a knowing. (Don't be disappointed if the actual guidance doesn't jump out at you during the quiet time. It's more apt to show up unexpectedly at some later moment.) Meditation is getting on God's wavelength. Like listening to a radio, we tune in to God's presence. Simply feeling and enjoying the Presence is the only true purpose of meditation. With practice it becomes easier.

How to Meditate

How do you meditate? One way is to sit in a comfortable chair, with your feet flat on the floor and your hands resting in your lap. Close your eyes and take a few slow, easy breaths. Let each part of your body relax and "melt" into a restful feeling until you are in a state of quiet receptivity.

Now gently move your attention to an awareness of God's presence all around you and in you. Feel the joy of knowing that you are one with God and that there are no limits on your life. The more you meditate, the more you will find yourself sensing God's great love for you and for all creation.

Begin today to set aside some time to meditate—to rest in God's presence. Make it a daily habit. This Presence wants you to know It, so use your meditation periods to open your soul to this gift-of-all-gifts.

SPECIAL NOTE: You'll find after prayer and meditation become an established habit with you, the two will begin to merge until eventually your quiet time is devoted solely to waiting in the Presence. Sitting quietly and simply waiting in silence enables us more and more to bring the feelings of our oneness with God out into our daily activities. And this, of course, is what really counts.

Once Over Lightly–

- Prayer is any conscious attempt to experience more of the presence of God.
- Any way that someone expresses a desire to feel the presence of God is a legitimate prayer.
- When you pray, something happens to change *you.*
- Spending time in prayer opens your heart so God can work freely *through* you.
- Meditation is getting on God's wavelength.
- Eventually your prayer/meditation time will be devoted solely to waiting in the Presence.

The Wheels

"It is not well for a man to pray cream and live skim-milk."

– Henry Ward Beecher

Have you talked to God lately? When you are "talking" to God, you are obviously making a conscious attempt to experience more of God's presence. This, then, is a form of prayer. When you talk to God, whether out loud or silently, God is always ready to listen to you, always ready to meet you at the secret place of the Most High. The best part is that you can go there anytime you want to.

What do you talk to God about? You might want to tell God how your life is going or how you feel about things. Speak to God as if you were speaking to your very best and closest friend, because God is. There is no secret too secret to tell God. There is nothing you cannot share. You can trust God completely with your most private and special thoughts and feelings. There is no problem too difficult for God to solve. When you are truly open to God's guidance, you will always be given the perfect idea so that you can work out your problem in the best possible way.

Ponder Point

There is strong evidence from prayer ministries such as Silent Unity, which receives millions of prayer requests each year, that praying for others "works." But how can it if prayer is our own individual attempt to experience more of the presence of God? When we pray for others, aren't we really trying to manipulate God into doing something for someone else?

But the object of praying for others is not to be fixed on a specific outcome. Rather it is to see that individual as open to God's will, and to affirm for him or her the highest blessing. So if a man asks for your prayers that he might marry a certain woman, your prayers should acknowledge his specific request but at the same time should affirm that he might marry the *right* woman. If someone wanted prayers to win the lottery, your prayers should be for "this or something better," that the person might become aware of the great abundance already available. Perhaps winning the lottery would not be best for that person. We've all heard stories about some people's lives turning sour after winning huge amounts of money.

Does this mean we should never pray for what we feel is best for us? No, it's okay to pray for specific things, as long as we're open to the greater flow of God's blessings in our lives, which, by the way, just might *not* include our specific "thing."

Warm-Ups

1. Often what we pray for may not be the best thing for us. *Can you think of any examples in your life when you prayed for something you did not get and later were glad your prayers were not answered?*

2. We said that God will give you the perfect idea "so that you can work out your problem in the best possible way." *Contrast this with the concept of praying to God so that God will take care of things for us.*

Going for It

It's been said that if you floss your teeth for one solid month, you will do it forever . . . This says something about it taking that long for a new habit to become permanent.

Try this experiment: *Meditate every day for a full month. Choose a time each day or evening to sit still, become quiet, and allow the presence of God to fill your heart and mind. See if, after thirty days of this, meditation develops into a lifetime habit.*

Chapter 10

Who Is Jesus?

The Wisdom

Not just another
pretty face.

He bled when cut; he hurt when bruised. He laughed, he cried, he got angry, he loved. He had feelings and emotions like every other human being. Jesus was a man, fully human in *every* respect. His life is important to us for one towering reason: *He discovered he was one with God.* He somehow sensed the force of God within him and, because he sensed it, knew all things were possible.

Understanding God so perfectly, Jesus was able to do things throughout his lifetime that seemed like miracles to those who witnessed them. Yet he taught that we, too, can do all he did— "in fact, will do greater works than these" (Jn. 14:12)—because the power and presence of God is just as surely in us as it was in him. This is the most critically important teaching of Jesus.

Jesus showed us how to experience God's presence. He showed us how to think, to pray, to act. And his teachings are timeless—just as valid for us today as they were for his followers two millennia ago.

Contrary to what doctrines have evolved in many organized religions over the last two thousand years, Jesus never intended that people worship *him*. His intention was that we do as he did and worship God: "Worship the Lord your God, and serve only him" (Lk. 4:8).

Not Impossible for Us

When you read about Jesus and the awe-inspiring things he did, some of them seem almost impossible for the rest of us to do. Yet as incredible as Jesus' life may seem, the fact is that what one human being (Jesus) can do, any human being (you) can do! If we follow Jesus' teachings and the examples of his life, we will be able to know our oneness with God just as he did. And when we do, we'll be able to elevate ourselves into a new spiritual realm, just as he did.

Jesus is our Way Shower because his teachings and his life can show *us* the way. His teachings on humility, on loving each other, on loving God—which he referred to (in RSV) as "the great commandment"—and on forgiveness are all part of a spiritual road map for us to follow. And it all begins with knowing God lives through us and as us, and then responding to life in a loving manner. Jesus discovered that . . . and so can we. Despite all obstacles, it *is* possible.

Once Over Lightly–

- Jesus was fully human in every respect.
- Jesus is important to us because he was like us and he was able to discover his oneness with God.
- He taught that all humans can do what he did.
- His teachings are timeless—as valid today as two thousand years ago.
- Jesus intended people to worship God, not him.
- Jesus is our Way Shower.

The Wheels

"To escape criticism—do nothing, say nothing, be nothing."

—Elbert Hubbard

Whenever there is talk of Jesus, the emphasis is usually on his divinity and seldom on his humanity. Yet his humanity is the bottom line to our understanding of his life and any lessons we can glean from it. After all, if Jesus were not fully human, how could we identify with him? How could he be our Way Shower? What hope could we ever have of achieving what he did? If he were not *fully* human, he would simply be one more religious icon to be admired but kept on a shelf.

Ponder Point

When golf balls were first manufactured, their surface covers were made smooth. But gradually it became obvious that the balls which got roughed up through use would go farther and straighter than the new, smooth ones. So the manufacturers began turning out the "dimpled" covers we see on golf balls today.

Everything traveling through life gets roughed up in one way or another. (If you've read about his life, you know Jesus was no exception.) But we can take those rough spots in our lives, turn them around, and use them to our advantage. The trials and agonies we go through, if dealt with from a perspective of love and forgiveness, will enable us to go the extra distance—just like the golf balls.

Warm-Ups

You no doubt know people who are considered street-smart. How would you like to become "Jesus-smart?" You can begin by practicing doing as Jesus did. Let's say, for example, your feelings are hurt because you feel someone gave you a dirty deal or said something hurtful to you. Instead of your usual reaction—pouting, getting angry, or whatever—ask yourself, "What would Jesus do in this situation?" It could be you'll think Jesus would feel another person's obnoxious behavior is *that* person's problem, not his. What if someone around you is really abusive or dangerous? What would Jesus do in that situation?

For an entire week, try to feel how Jesus would act in any situation you find yourself in. Once you've de-

cided, act that way yourself. Describe one of these situations.

Going for It

When was the last time you read some of Jesus' words? Read one of the four gospels in the New Testament. (It's especially helpful, and easier, to read a red-letter edition that features Jesus' words in red.) Don't hurry through it. Read it slowly so that you get the real message behind each story Jesus tells. Ask yourself: "How does this story apply in my own life? What is Jesus saying to *me?*" *Write down your experience.*

Chapter 11

Who or What Is the Christ?

The Wisdom

Christ is your real last name.

You have different sets of clothes and each change of clothes gives you a different look. Yet no matter what clothes you put on, you are still you. Perhaps it will help to think of your Christ Self in a similar way—*it* doesn't change, either, no matter how many different ways you look or act on the outside. The real you—that Christ Self—is always perfect and makes you the one-of-a-kind individual you are. The Christ is the presence of God in each of us. (Does this definition of the Christ have a familiar ring to it? Ten points if you guessed that your Spirit and the Christ are the same thing.)

It's our responsibility as creations of God to express our Christ Selves. In fact, it is our *only* responsibility because if we do this, we will be loving, compassionate, forgiving, gracious, joy-filled, and *all* the other things that are part of our divine design. In allowing the world to see the splendor of our divinity, we become way showers, as Jesus was. And also like Jesus, we'll recognize this same Christ nature in everyone else.

The Christ: Your Real Self

"Christ" is not Jesus' last name. Jesus was able to reveal so completely his Christ Self—his God nature—that he was called Jesus Christ. But actually Christ is as much *your* real name too. The word *Christ* comes from the Greek word *Christos*, meaning "the anointed." "Christ" is a title reserved for anyone who becomes aware of and fully realizes the depths of his or her divine possibilities, as Jesus did. Christ is God individualized in each of us. The Christ is not a person. *Jesus* is the person. The Christ refers to the spiritual aspect of him—and of you and of all people. Jesus and the Christ—there is a difference.

Once Over Lightly–

- The real you—your Christ Self—is always perfect.
- The Christ is the presence of God in each of us.
- It is your responsibility to express your Christ Self.

The Wheels

"Enlightenment doesn't care how you get there."

—Thaddeus Golas

Siddhartha Gautama was called Buddha (the Enlightened One), but "the Enlightened One" was not his last name. It was a description. Jesus is called "the Christ" or "Jesus Christ," but Christ is not his last name. It is a description.

Ponder Point

Jesus was the man who discovered and expressed his divinity and became known as Jesus Christ. So here's the buzz: *Since we were created with the exact same potential as Jesus, we, too, can discover and express our divinity. We, too, can become "the Christ."* The more you ponder this statement, the more awesome it becomes. Allow the impact of its meaning to filter down into your soul, where it can do its work.

Warm-Ups

In the preceding chapter we contrasted being street-smart with being "Jesus-smart"—doing as Jesus would in every situation. How about taking it one step further and being "Christ-smart"? How about filtering all situations, encounters, and interactions through your own indwelling Christ Self before determining your course of action? After all, the Christ in you is the same Christ that was in Jesus. Things equal to the same thing are equal to each other.

Taking the example in Chapter 10, your feelings have been hurt because of what someone did or said to you. Instead of your usual reaction—pouting, getting angry, or whatever—it was suggested you ask yourself, "What would Jesus do in this situation?" This time ask yourself, "What would the Christ—the divine part of me—do?"

For an entire week, try to feel how you would act in any particular situation you find yourself in if you acted only from your Christ Self. Once you've decided, do your best to act that way yourself. Describe one of these situations.

Going for It

The Christ in each of us is unquestionably what makes us one of a kind. Your divine nature is forever drawing you toward your unique gift, something you are better at than anyone else. Maybe you're not the best algebra student. But maybe you're the best computer-chess player. Or maybe the best photographer. Or roller blader. Or handler of injured animals. Everybody excels at *something.*

Give some thought to your own unique gift. Have you discovered what it is? If not, keep searching. And once you do discover it, begin to think of ways you can use it to make your world a better one. Your Christ Self loves to be shared with others.

Chapter 12

What Is the Holy Spirit?

The Wisdom

Meet one of life's greatest secrets.

By now it's no secret to you that no matter how great an idea may be, it goes nowhere until you actually do something about it. It works the same with God. God's ideas must be expressed in the world, and it is the Holy Spirit that does this work. The Holy Spirit is the moving force that makes God's plan happen. It is the aspect of God that created the universe and each of us.

But let's not make the mistake of thinking of the Holy Spirit as something separate from God, because It isn't. If you have the idea to paint a picture and then you actually paint the picture, who does the work? It's still you—you as both idea and doer. Same with the Holy Spirit. It's the aspect of God that does the work, but It's still God.

One of Life's Greatest Secrets

The Holy Spirit aspect of God provides you with all your creative ideas, and it is the Holy Spirit aspect of God that keeps you alive. So it's safe to say the Holy Spirit is *God in action*.

Since it's the job of the Holy Spirit to *do* things, to *create* things, It's programmed to be active in your life to make things better for you. Spirit wants to improve every facet of your life. And there is nothing the Holy Spirit loves more than to be appreciated and called upon for help. Oh, how Spirit loves this, because then It can do what It was created to do, which is to make new and wonderful things for you. And *new* is the operative word here.

IMPORTANT FACT: This creative ability of the Holy Spirit can create *new* things, *new* conditions, *new* circumstances in your mind, your body, and the situations of your life. Since Its very nature is to be creative, It is not limited by what was in the past. The Holy Spirit can change *anything* . . . when we cooperate with It. WOW!

This is one of life's greatest secrets, and if you understand it, your own life will be unimaginably blessed. The Holy Spirit will see to it!

Once Over Lightly—

- The Holy Spirit is God in action.
- The work of the Holy Spirit is to make new and wonderful things for you.
- The Holy Spirit is not limited by what was in the past. It can change *anything*.

The Wheels

"May the Force be with you."

—Ben (Obi-Wan) Kenobi, Star Wars

Jesus had hoped his apostles would go out and perform the kinds of healings he himself did. But they became discouraged by their failure to replicate the Master's acts. Something was missing.

In Acts, we read that sometime after Jesus was no longer with them, some of the apostles who had gathered with the faithful suddenly had a transformative experience: "All of them were filled with the Holy Spirit and began to speak in other languages, as the Spirit gave them ability" (Acts 2:4). Chapter 3 of Acts goes on to describe an astounding healing Peter and John were able to facilitate after this experience. Peter, who had once been shy and unsure of himself, now acted with boldness and assurance. When people "saw the boldness of Peter and John and realized that they were uneducated and ordinary men, they were amazed and recognized them as companions of Jesus" (Acts 4:13).

Ponder Point

God in action—the Holy Spirit—is a living, active Force. Restlessly pursuing people through whom It can work, It is eternally on the move. Like a strong wind that blows this way and that, the Holy Spirit seeks openings where It can get in. Let's be continually open to this Force as It comes knocking at the doors of our hearts. We can then seize the opportunity to become bold, like Peter and John, and master any situation we might face. With the power of the Holy Spirit active in us, we, too, will amaze people.

Warm-Ups

Evidence of the work of the Holy Spirit is all around you. Begin now to train your eyes to see more of it and your ears to hear more of it. *How many examples can you find of the Holy Spirit at work around you? Describe them.*

Going for It

The work of the Holy Spirit weaves its way from one generation to the next, linking us all together. *Make an appointment with an elderly relative (a grandparent, for example) or friend. Interview this person about the past—the times in which he or she grew up. How did world events influence this individual's life? What were the significant personal events of his or her life? What info about the past did you learn? How does it relate to your life today?*

Chapter 13

What About the Bible?

The Wisdom

Read the complete
story of your life.

Menelik II, emperor of Ethiopia from 1889–1913, displayed one eccentric behavior. He was absolutely sure that eating some pages of the Bible when he felt unwell would improve his health. Throughout the years, a small biblical intake did not hurt him. However, in 1913 when feeling very sick and recovering from a stroke, he ordered that the whole book of Kings be ripped from the Bible and fed him one page at a time. The emperor died before consuming all the pages.

It was Sir Francis Bacon, in the sixteenth century, who said some books are meant to be "chewed and digested," but we don't think he intended his words to be taken literally!

The Bible does certainly require "digesting," however. Made up of 66 separate books, it was written over centuries by many people who contemplated the wonders of God. Although the Bible is a record of historical events and a collection of legends from different civilizations, it is far more than that. The Bible is especially important to us because, when it is interpreted personally, it is a record of our individual search for God.

For example, as we begin to realize we are one with God, we automatically express more of our Christ Selves and gradually wake up to the fact that God is within us. From the Old to the New Testament, we start out like Adam, who was not aware of his Christ Self, and we work toward becoming like Jesus, who fully recognized his oneness with God. Beginning with Adam and ending with the Christ, the Bible is really the record of our own spiritual progress. That's why when we read the Bible we should try to look past the obvious story to discover what it is saying to *us* at a deeper level.

Meanings Behind Words

The stories and events of the Bible are symbols of what happens in our own lives. The Bible, therefore, can mean something different to each person. As you read it you will discover how every story contains aspects of your own character.

Reading it this way, looking for how it applies to our own lives, is called interpreting the Bible *metaphysically*—looking behind the words for the real ideas and what they represent to us personally. (We'll get more specific about this in the ***Wheels*** section.)

Some people think the Bible is an old, outdated, boring book. Old, yes. Boring, in some parts. Outdated, never—not when we personalize it by interpreting it metaphysically. *Then* it provides up-to-the-minute insights into our thoughts and behaviors. Then it is continually new and fresh.

When you read the Bible this way, it always has something new to say specifically to *you*. Layers and layers of meaning are there for you to discover. And you'll notice that as *you* change and evolve, the meanings in the Bible stories change as well. A living book and not some outdated collection of religious writings, the Bible will always have deep meaning for you because it contains the great truth about your world and about you personally. The Bible is a timeless book, the "Book of Life"—*your* life.

Once Over Lightly–

- The Bible is a record of your individual search for God.
- When you read the Bible, you should try to look past the obvious story to discover what it is saying to *you.*
- As you change and evolve, the meanings in the Bible stories change as well.

The Wheels

Q: *What does the story of Jonah and the great fish teach us?*

A: You can't keep a good man down.

Is the Bible the word of God? If we believe God "speaks" to us through ideas, then those whose words make up the Bible were inspired by God. Does that mean the Bible is the only book which contains God's words? No. All of the great religions believe their sacred writings are the word of God. And why not? Whoever is truly open to God's presence and ideas, and speaks or writes those ideas, is speaking the words of God.

Ponder Point

No matter how wonderful, sacred, or special anyone considers the Bible to be, unless it can help us to recognize more of the presence of God in our lives, it could even be called worthless. It would be like having great food you can't eat or piles of money you can't spend—just having it means nothing. Knowledge is great, but if you can't apply it, where is its value?

The Bible is full of obvious teachings on the importance of loving God and our neighbor, forgiveness, turning the other cheek, being humble, and many other essential concepts. But at the same time it is filled with more subtle messages directly applicable to our individual lives. For example, in Genesis 19:26, Lot's wife looks back at the cities of Sodom and Gomorrah and turns into a pillar of salt. Can't we apply this to our own lives? Okay, so when we look back, we don't literally turn into salt. But the more we concentrate on the past and recycle it, the more we become solidified in the past, destroying the present.

In Mark 14:66-72, Peter, afraid of being identified with Jesus, denies three times that he knows him. Have you ever denied the Christ in you when you've known what the right thing to do was but didn't do it because you were ashamed or afraid to in front of your friends?

What about the story in Mark 4:35-41 where Jesus, after a day of preaching, gets into a boat with his disciples and promptly falls asleep. Soon a fierce storm blows in and the disciples panic. Afraid for their lives, they awaken Jesus and ask him to calm the storm, which he does.

We all experience stormy periods in our lives. *Can you identify any "storms" that took place or are taking place in your life? Have you awakened the Christ in you to address these storms?*

Warm-Ups

Interpret one of these stories from the Bible and apply your interpretation to your own life:

Jonah and the whale (Jon. 1,2)

The tower of Babel (Gen. 11:1-9)

The woman hemorrhaging (Mk. 5:24-34)

Going for It

Check out some of the other sacred writings: the Islamic holy book, the Koran; the Hindu Bhagavad-Gita and the Upanishads; the ancient Buddhist sacred texts, the Pali Canon; the basic text of Taoism, the Tao Te Ching. *Do you feel they are inspired writings? Do you consider them to be as much God's words as the Bible?*

Chapter 14

Creating With Thoughts and Words

The Wisdom

Issue your royal decree
and watch what happens.

You are the royal ruler of your world! You have the authority over your life. *You* are in control.

Whoa . . . No way! I'm in control of nothing *in my life. Everyone else is in charge. My teachers, my parents, my coach . . . Even my dog has control over me. (Who has to take whom out whenever she stands at the door and barks?) Sorry, I don't buy this one.*

We understand how you feel—no kidding. It does seem as if we are the last ones to have any control over our own lives. And yet the simple truth is that no matter what the circumstances of your life are right now, you control your *thoughts* and that is what ultimately controls your life.

But, as with any ruler, along with power comes responsibility. Not only do you have to be willing to take command of your life, you also have to be willing to accept full responsibility for your decisions.

Thoughts and Words = Power

The power of your ruling ability lies mainly in two very important arenas: your thoughts and your words. Thoughts and words are the bricks and mortar with which you build your kingdom. They have creative power, and when you really *believe* what you think and say, your thoughts and words go forth as loyal subjects to do the bidding of their ruler, which is you!

History has shown us there can be good monarchs and not-so-good ones. Since the king or queen is in complete command of the kingdom, the assistants must obey orders at all times. If the ruler issues a beneficial command, the result will be positive. If it's a poor command, the results will be less than desirable. The command is always carried out exactly according to the royal decree.

Your thoughts and words act in the same way as a royal decree. They go forth to create with your royal power. You, as supreme ruler of your thoughts and words, have total command over what direction they take. A negative or destructive thought can always be replaced by a positive, constructive thought. A negative or hurtful word can always be rendered powerless by speaking kind and positive words. It's as simple as that.

Ideally, our thoughts and words should reflect our *true* Selves—the Christ within us. The same power we sometimes use so destructively in our thoughts and words can be turned around and used constructively for *positive* results. You can command it. You are in charge of your life.

Once Over Lightly–

- You are in control of your thoughts and that is what ultimately controls your life.
- You must be willing to take responsibility for your decisions.
- Your thoughts and words have creative power. You have total command over what direction they take.

The Wheels

"Man does not live by words alone, despite the fact that sometimes he has to eat them."

—*Adlai Stevenson*

Thoughts and words are treated as one and the same in this chapter because they pretty much *are* the same. Although we may sometimes accuse people of not thinking before they speak (or perhaps we've been accused of it ourselves!), this is not accurate because words are actually crystalized thoughts, so we *always* think before we speak. Our words are our thoughts that have been distilled and concentrated so that we can express them to others. (When you think about it, you realize words actually allow people to read our minds—at least those portions of our minds that we want them to read.)

But there's more to words than that. Words have power, *real* power. It's amazing to realize that just by speaking words, people can be made to laugh and cry, to feel excited and motivated, to feel angry or depressed, peaceful or fearful. Our own words can affect us in the same way.

Ponder Point

It's one thing to think a thought such as "Who could ever love a jerk like me?" but when we actually articulate it, it shocks the body with its stark power. Self-talk has the same effect on an individual as talk from another person. Maybe even more since when we speak, we have an audience of 100 trillion cells listening. It's the largest audience we will ever speak to. And each cell is attentive to our wishes. The more we hear a thought expressed, in silence or as words, the more we will try, either consciously or unconsciously, to make it a self-fulfilling prophecy.

Warm-Ups

The title of this chapter is "Creating With Thoughts and Words." The compelling word here is *creating* because we can dramatically alter our lives by redirecting our thinking. What you have created in your life with your thoughts and words you can also re-create.

1. *Exactly what aspect of your life would you like to re-create? What aspect of your life would you like to change?*

2. Keeping in mind that the law of cause and effect is always at work, what specific thoughts and words can you begin thinking and saying to yourself which will start this change?

Going for It

This little exercise may be a bit of a pain in the neck to do because it involves writing throughout the day in a small notebook. But it's well worth the effort.

For one full week, keep a record of all the times you belittle yourself in thoughts or words. Create two columns—a positive one and a negative one. Every time you think a negative thought about yourself, make a note of it. Every time you speak a negative word about yourself, make a note of it. Do the same for the positive thoughts and words you think and say about yourself.

At the end of a week, compare your negative and positive scores. You may be surprised.

Chapter 15

Yes and No

The Wisdom

Check out your garden—
weeds or flowers?

A man who for decades had a morbid fear of thunder finally went to a famous psychiatrist who specialized in treating brontophobia (fear of thunder).

The doctor scolded him for being childish, telling him it was time to grow up. "How can you be afraid of thunder? It's your friend. Think of it merely as the heavens playing drums. It's all in your mind, you know."

"And that will cure my phobia?" questioned the man.

"Well, try it. And if it doesn't," replied the doctor, "do as I do. Stuff big wads of cotton in your ears, crawl under the bed, and sing 'Yankee Doodle' as loud as you can."

That wacko psychiatrist didn't get it quite right, but it's true that everything does begin in the mind. The mind is the storehouse for our feelings, thoughts, and beliefs about people and things. And we know that, since everything works according to the law, whatever we have in our minds will eventually show up in our world. This is because the mind is the soil in which we grow our world.

So you can see how important it is to "plant" the right things. It's also important to have the right soil if your garden is going to grow the way you'd like it to. If you want flowers, you first have to pull the weeds; otherwise, they'll crowd out the flowers and prevent them from growing there. Weeds can crowd out the flowers of your mind too. The "weeds" in your mind could be stuff like hate, fear, jealousy, resentment, selfishness, or anything else getting in the way of your being the person you are supposed to be.

Release

We can get rid of "mind weeds" by using statements of release. These are statements that deny the accuracy and power of any negative, harmful, untrue beliefs we have. Some weeds in a garden can act as if they own the place. They look beautiful and can fool us into believing they are flowers.

Negative situations can brazenly act the same way. They fool us into believing they are true. But they are hollow, and actually powerless over us if we can remember to look for this truth: There is only God, and God is all-powerful.

Examples of a release statement:

I am not afraid.

I am not a poor student.

Hey, fear, get out of my life!

You can make up your own release statement for any situation that seems to be overshadowing God. There's nothing complicated or mysterious about release statements. They are simply a way of saying, "No! Not wanted in my soul!" In fact, the word *No!* itself is a very powerful release. When spoken with conviction, it can snap you immediately back on track. Like any good release statement, it has the ability to cancel out the negative. Your mind may be screaming, "I just *know* I'm going to flunk this exam." Well . . . scream "No!" right back at it.

When you come up with a good, strong "No" statement to fit your situation, use it many times a day—as often as necessary. Say it aloud when you can, and say it silently whenever you think of it. This is a way you can pull those weeds that have to be gotten rid of before you can plant your garden. "No! I will *not* flunk this exam."

But what would happen if you got rid of all those weeds that have been hindering you and you didn't do anything else with your garden? Pretty soon those pesky weeds would be springing up again. Once we pull the weeds, the soil must be planted with something to take their place—with flowers.

Our minds work the same way. After we've done the releasing work, we then "plant the flowers" right away, before the weeds can return. We do this with what we call *affirmations.*

Affirmations

Affirmations are strong, *true* statements about ourselves or a situation. Since it's a fact that God is in every situation, the affirmation should reflect this. For instance, some affirmations could be:

I am intelligent.

I am well and strong.

I am filled with love.

I am calm and peaceful.

You can make up affirmations to fit your own needs.

An affirmation is a way of saying, "Yes!" The only rules to follow are that your affirmation must be based on the reality that God is present and that it must not be contrary to God's laws. Then it works to establish whatever it is you are decreeing. It would do no good, for instance, to affirm that cigarettes are good for you when they work against God's laws for health. It would do no good to affirm that you cannot be hurt if you jump in front of a speeding train!

Get the principle—the main idea—behind affirmations? They *must* be based on what is true. But when they are, and when we use them over and over each day, they become powerful aids to improving ourselves and our circumstances. What kind of garden is your mind? Filled with weeds or filled with flowers? If your garden needs work, time to get busy with these two great tools—release and affirmation. "No!" and "Yes!"

Once Over Lightly–

- What you hold in your mind will eventually show up in your world.
- You can get rid of "mind weeds" by using statements of release.
- The negative needs to be replaced so there's no room for its return.
- Release statements have the ability to cancel out the negative.
- Affirmations are strong, *true* statements about yourself or a situation.

The Wheels

"Nothing is more difficult, and therefore more precious, than to be able to decide."

—Napoleon

Statements of release and affirmation—"No!" and "Yes!"—are two of the most powerful tools you can utilize to keep you on the path to receive God's blessings. Like mental training wheels, they work together to monitor your thoughts and keep you balanced.

Ponder Point

The essential aspect of both release and affirmation statements is that *they must be based on a true statement.* Appearances may indicate that you're stressed out from work or school. Yet the eternal you—the you that was created as a unique expression of God—can't possibly be stressed out. The eternal you was created in God's peace and is always immersed in God's peace. Ultimately, it is your inability to identify with this aspect of yourself that is causing the stress. So for you to release the stressed-out feelings by saying "I am *not* stressed out," or "Stress cannot affect me" may seem ludicrous at one level, yet it's quite true at your most basic level.

To affirm *I am peaceful and calm* in the midst of taking final exams or dealing with your love life in shambles or scrambling to meet a deadline may seem like the biggest lie you've ever told yourself. But at the level of Spirit, it's absolutely right on target.

Warm-Ups

Statements of release and affirmation don't do you any good if they're just filed away in your intellect. You have to *feel* the words. You have to hear yourself say them—either silently or out loud. It's hearing words connected to strong feelings that makes an impact.

• *Take a look at the part of your life that is in the most turmoil. Analyze your feelings about what's going on.*

• *Now make up a suitable release statement you can use throughout the day. Write it out.*

• *Next, make up a suitable affirmation you can use throughout the day. Write it out.*

• *Use both statements throughout the day as often as you can think of saying them—either silently or aloud.*

Going for It

The concept of release and affirmation is an ancient one. It's worked well for thousands and thousands of people throughout the centuries. Jesus himself advised, "Let your word be 'Yes, Yes' or 'No, No'" (Mt. 5:37).

What are your feelings about the concept? Are statements of release and affirmation still workable today? We characterized them as mental "training wheels." But training wheels on a bicycle are abandoned once the rider gains his or her balance. *Does this hold true for release and affirmation statements?*

Chapter 16

Always a Blessing

The Wisdom

Get out the shovel and start digging—it's there.

Scott Rolen's arm was broken by a pitched ball in 1996, his first year with the Phillies. He was really angry at the pitcher who hit him. But the next year, Scott was the unanimous choice for the National League "Jackie Robinson Rookie of the Year" award. The irony is that he wouldn't have been eligible for this honor had his arm not been broken the year before. At the time he was injured, Rolen had 130 at-bats, the maximum a player can have to keep his rookie status. So the next year Rolen was officially considered a rookie again and therefore was eligible for the prestigious award. "I wasn't very happy with him [Steve Trachsel, the pitcher who broke his arm] then," Rolen said. "But it might be a good time to give him a call and thank him" (*USA Today*, Nov. 5, 1997, p. 16C).

COSMIC NEWS BULLETIN: *There's always a blessing*. If this seems 180 degrees from reality, it's because we're in the habit of judging situations and people in our lives as "good" and "bad."

Maybe it's difficult to think of having a broken leg or the measles, getting failing grades, or being robbed as having a blessing in it. But it does—somewhere and somehow a blessing is present. This has to be true because *God* is always present.

So how do we deal with something appearing to be less than "good"? The first step is to remember that God is everywhere and that in the grand scheme of the universe, God is working on our behalf. Next, we start looking for God in the situation; we start looking for the blessing. If we look patiently enough, we will always find it.

Sometimes the blessing does not show itself right away, so we have to trust God's plan. Eventually we'll find the blessing and see how something we thought was "bad" really brought some "good" into our lives and the world.

For Instance

Let's have some more, real-life examples of what might seem to be negative situations. An unhappy, overweight woman who broke her leg became so impressed with the exercises to strengthen the muscles that she started on a total-fitness program and eventually found herself much happier as a slimmer, healthier person.

A young boy at home in bed with measles watched a daytime television program on oceanography. He became so fascinated with the subject that he later made it his career.

A young man flunked out of college. He had never studied and had gone to college only to please his parents. After several years of worldly experience and "growing up," he returned to college because *he* wanted to attend. As a more mature student he was able to choose a degree program that really excited him, and he got much more out of college than he ever would have as a teenager. He appreciated his education, graduated with honors, and was hired by a company he wouldn't have dreamed of applying to had he graduated on his original schedule.

And here's our personal favorite—a widow whose house was burglarized later married the police investigator on her case!

It's not always easy to find the blessing in what at the time seems like a devastating situation. But as time passes and we remember God is present no matter what, we give the blessing a chance to emerge and we see how things worked out in a different but "right" way.

Once Over Lightly–

- If you look patiently enough, you'll always find a blessing in every situation.
- God's blessing may not be so obvious at first.
- God is present, no matter what.

The Wheels

"I'm such an optimist I'd go after Moby Dick in a rowboat and take the tartar sauce with me."

–Zig Ziglar

The death of their children by drunken drivers prompted a group of mothers to found the organization MADD—*Mothers Against Drunk Driving.* This organization has done more to stiffen the laws against drunk driving than perhaps any other single group. As a result, it has saved countless lives.

Were the deaths of their children worth the gains made in public awareness of the problem and the subsequent laws passed to address it and the thousands of lives saved because of it? We seriously doubt there's one mother who would be willing to trade her child's life for all of the gains made by MADD. But, *given the fact of their children's deaths by people under the influence of alcohol or other drugs,* these mothers were then willing to allow whatever blessings that would come out of the experience to unfold.

That's the lesson for us. If something has happened in our lives that we can't change, then we simply have to accept it. But we don't stop there. Let's go on to also accept any residual blessings the situation presents to us. While often hidden, blessings are *always* there. It's a matter of opening ourselves to them. Slogging around in depression, resentment, and hurt feelings is definitely not the way to go if we're looking for blessings.

Ponder Point

Life is really a series of learning points. Everything we do gives us feedback. We adjust our lives according to the feedback we receive, and this adjustment either blesses us or gets us into more trouble. For instance, we learn at a very early age that touching a hot stove gives us great pain. The obvious blessing is that we do not again deliberately touch a hot stove. Just as important, we do all in our power to make sure that no one else does. But even further, having experienced any kind of pain ourselves, (unless we are mentally unbalanced) we do all in our power to make sure no one else suffers *any* pain—either physical or emotional.

Warm-Ups

As we've said, there's no situation or person so "bad" that God is not present. *Look back at some of the things in your past that seemed so terrible when they happened, and try to identify what good came out of them. How are those situations blessing you now?*

Going for It

Here's a tough one. There have been some first-class villains in history. One thinks of Genghis Khan, Attila the Hun, Adolf Hitler, Saddam Hussein—none of whom you'd call Mr. Nice Guy! *Choose one villain and make a list of the blessings that have come about because of him or her.*

Chapter 17

Act—Don't React!

The Wisdom

"It's not my table,"
said the waiter.

Here's the deal: It usually isn't so much what people say or do to us which causes our hurts; it's more a case of how we *react* which allows us to be hurt. If someone says something you don't like, his anger (or jealousy or whatever) is *his* problem—not yours. You always have the option of not accepting it or letting it bother you. Now this is the way it's *supposed* to be, of course. The ultimate goal is not even to be disappointed in people or let our feelings be hurt by them. But who of us is there yet?

Still, it *is* possible. We can begin by taking baby steps in that direction. For instance, we can once again remind ourselves that God is present in every situation. That way we won't get as upset or angry if something seems to go wrong. The waiter who receives complaints from another waiter's table knows "it's not my table." He may listen courteously as the customers bad-mouth the other waiter and the restaurant, but he does not let their negative comments about someone else's service affect *him*.

When we look to other people or things to make us happy, we put our hopes and expectations in the wrong place—we put them "out there." Only one place can bring us lasting happiness, and that is inside ourselves. When we learn to turn to our Christ Selves, we will *never* be disappointed. Our sense of spirituality is the only thing we can rely on, because it is unchangingly right. HELPFUL REMINDER: Prayer and meditation can help us here, because they keep us tuned in to our true Selves. Otherwise, it's too easy to get thrown off track.

If you've been reacting to everyone and everything in your world, giving all of it permission to affect you, it doesn't have to be that way. If you want to change this, look to your own Christ nature as your source of peace and happiness. It makes a difference.

This doesn't mean we ignore others or are unkind to them. No way. It means we practice loving everyone and seeing God at work everywhere. It means always doing our best. When we do, we've done our share, and that is all *we* have to worry about. What others do and say is *their* responsibility—not ours.

Here again, we'll present the ideal—what we're all aiming for—so bear with us for a minute. The grouchy supermarket clerk, the rude waiter, the schoolyard bully, the selfish friend—they really don't have anything to do with *you*. Each is doing what he or she feels must be done at the time. The bottom line is that those words and actions should have no effect on you, because they really are not about you. They're about that person's own problems and what's going on inside. *Your* job is a B-I-G one—to do your best. To the best of your ability, think, speak, and act from your Christ Self, which loves everyone and sees the Christ in everyone else.

It doesn't take a genius to figure out that people *do* hurt us. Physically, especially, people can hurt us. If this is the case, make tracks as fast as possible to get away from the danger. Yet as you do, you still have to recognize the divinity hidden somewhere deep within that person.

A tough lesson for some of us to learn, this acting-instead-of-reacting business. But getting a handle on it is a life changer. How could it not be? We've taken back from others the power to impact our own lives in ways we do not want. In reclaiming our power, *we* get to decide how we respond to life.

Once Over Lightly–

- It isn't so much what people say or do to you which causes hurt as it is your *reaction* to them which allows you to be hurt.
- The ultimate goal is not to be disappointed in people or let your feelings be hurt by them.
- What others do or say is *their* responsibility—not yours.

The Wheels

If one person calls you a jackass, pay no attention to him. But if five people call you one, go out and buy yourself a saddle.

–Arabian proverb

When we allow the opinion or actions of others to affect us negatively—when we *re*act— we have given away the most precious gift that God has given us. We've given away our free will. By allowing others to control us, we have surrendered the responsibility and the privilege of being in control of our own lives. Hey, if we're going to give away our free will, let's at least give it to God!

Ponder Point

Acting instead of reacting is simple, but it's far from easy. In other words, the theory is simple but the practice of it is difficult, since we've gotten so out of the habit.

In theory, what could be simpler than directing your own life and not letting anyone make you do what you don't want to do? (After all, you don't let someone else steer when you're driving your car.) But somehow we allow people to get us angry or frustrated or stressed. Maybe they remind us of areas in our own lives that need improvement or weaknesses we perceive in ourselves which we think no one else sees. Or maybe we think they won't like us or accept us if we don't react as we have been. Whatever it is, *acting* rather than *re*acting is a constant challenge. But we're born with the ability to do it. We just have to keep plugging away at it. The more occasions we catch ourselves reacting, especially destructively, the more we'll be able to change our responses and actions to God-centered positive ones.

Warm-Ups

Is there anyone in your life who really pushes your buttons? Someone in your family who only has to say certain words or assume a certain attitude to get you boiling? Someone at school or at work? Choose one person who directs his or her comments or actions toward you and affects you in the most negative way. Whoever this person is, *analyze why you react as you do to him or her. Next, make specific plans to begin responding in a different way, a more positive way, one more in keeping with your staying in charge of the situation rather than allowing this person to call all the shots.* (Remember, make the plans *specific*. "I'll try to do better" is not a specific plan.)

Going for It

We've all used expressions like "he gets me so mad" or "she gets me so frustrated" or "he gives me a pain in the neck." But wouldn't it be more accurate to say, "I *allow* him to get me so mad," or "I *allow* frustration to build in me when I deal with her" or "I *give myself* a pain in the neck when I react to him"?

Make a list of the expressions you use to describe your relationships with the people in your life whom you allow to upset you. Rewrite each phrase you use in a more "accurate" version. How you've been allowing people to affect you may surprise you.

Chapter 18

Judge Not

The Wisdom

Watch for the
waving red flag.

Ever notice that whenever you say something unkind about somebody you have an uneasy feeling deep inside afterwards? It's as if a big red flag waved within you and said, "Uh, uh." That feeling is your own Christ Self perpetually urging you to be more loving. And condemning others is not being loving.

Let's back up for a minute. We know God is everywhere—in all places and in all people. Each person has a Christ Self, which is perfect because it's the part tuned into its oneness with God. So if we condemn someone, we are actually condemning . . . oh, oh . . . a part of *God*.

Let's realize that it's a full-time job taking care

of our *own* thoughts and words and actions. What others do is *their* responsibility. Each person is doing what he or she believes is best, and it's not our job to criticize if it seems to us someone is on the wrong track.

We Don't Know What's Best for Others

We cannot possibly know what's best for anyone other than ourselves. (*That's* difficult enough!) God is working through everyone, and we have no right to judge harshly or to condemn. We don't like it when others do it to us, and we shouldn't do it to them.

This is one of the major teachings of Jesus (and other great spiritual teachers). He told us not to judge others. If we do, we're setting ourselves up for some huge speed bumps on our path.

Try to become aware of each time you're about to criticize someone, then catch it with a "Gotcha" and stop before you do. After you get the hang of catching yourself—and this not only takes months and months of practice usually, but it's also a never-ending job—you'll treasure those moments when you start seeing God in everyone.

Once Over Lightly–

- Your Christ Self urges you to be more loving. Condemning others is not being loving.
- If you condemn someone, you are condemning a part of God.
- What others do is their responsibility.
- You cannot possibly know what's best for anyone other than yourself.

The Wheels

"How would you like a job where, if you make a mistake, a big red light goes on and eighteen thousand people boo?"

—Jacques Plante, former hockey goalie

There's a world of difference between being judgmental and using your judgment. For example, someone at a party becomes obnoxious and belligerent after using drugs or drinking too much alcohol. Being *judgmental* would be to think of that person as an inferior jerk or as a weak-willed bully or any number of other pronouncements to tag him or her as unworthy of you.

On the other hand, using your *judgment* you would look at the person's actions and then judge the *actions* as harmful or dangerous. You might use your judgment still further to remove yourself from that person's company as long as he or she is using drugs. Many of us have friends who do drugs and who often try to include us in their habit: "Hey, this is great stuff. Give it a try!" It's okay to judge these people's drug use as dangerous and not to want to be with them. In fact, it's a good idea to keep away from them. But in removing yourself from them, don't judge them. Be clear in your own mind that it is not *they* you judge as unworthy of your involvement; it's their harmful actions only.

Ponder Point

Using your judgment and being judgmental are tough to separate. It's so easy to interfere in the life of someone you care about by becoming judgmental of his or her actions. Well, resist the temptation—back off.

Here . . . this may clarify things. You take a specific route to school or work every day. But everyone else in school or work gets there too. They take different routes, obviously, because they start from different spots. In the same way, your spiritual path has taken you one way, while other people's will take them another way. It's because we all start from different spots. Those using alcohol or other drugs are on their own path. It may not be your path, but it's the one they're on, so obviously it's up to them to get off it. Your job is not to judge them, only to love them. (We are not in conflict with each other; we are in conflict with our *perception* of each other.)

Warm-Ups

No doubt there have been times in your life when you were judgmental. How about the time someone cut you off in traffic or took the parking space you were about to pull into? What about the person who began smoking in the nonsmoking section of the restaurant or the one who got into the six-items-or-less-only line with a shopping cart full of groceries? Those are the easy ones to address. What gets really difficult is when someone physically harms you or a loved one, or deprives you of your money or a job promotion. They are the tough ones to deal with.

Take inventory of some actions in the past that you dealt with in a judgmental way. How could you have changed your response?

What about the present? Address the judgmental attitudes you have now. How can you separate the action from the person involved?

Going for It

Celebrities and politicians are always being accused of dastardly deeds. Seems they are forever being judged as nice or not-so-nice people based on what they have done. Of course, it's difficult to know what the real facts are because, especially in the "scandal sheets," so many facts can be grossly distorted to make the story more interesting.

Why do you think the popular press has a need to constantly offer negative publicity about celebrities?

Chapter 19

Don't Sweat It—Forget It

The Wisdom

Ta-da! Introducing the miracle worker.

At the age of fifteen, Adolph Coors IV was suddenly wrenched into heartbreak. His beloved father, Adolph Coors III, was kidnapped and held for ransom in February 1960. His body was finally discovered seven months later on an isolated hillside. He had been shot. For many years Coors seethed with hatred for Joseph Corbett, the man sentenced to life imprisonment for killing his father.

In 1975 Adolph Coors IV withdrew from the family brewing business, but he could not withdraw from his consuming hatred for Corbett. He prayed for help, because he was aware that his intense hatred was suffocating his experience of God's presence as well as affecting his relationship with people. Finally one day, surrendering to God's presence and power in him, Coors went to the Colorado penitentiary where Corbett was imprisoned; he hoped to visit with the man. Corbett refused to see him, however, and Coors left him a Bible inscribed with this message: "I'm here to see you today and I'm sorry that we could not meet. . . . I do forgive you, and I ask you to forgive me for the hatred I've held in my heart for you." Later Coors said that he actually had "a love for that man"—a love which could have only been put there by God.

Wipe the Slate Clean

Never go to sleep at night feeling angry or resentful toward anyone. Make it a habit to wipe the slate clean each evening so no bad feelings fester during the night, only to infect the next day.

If we feel we have to forgive someone, it means we judged him or her harshly. If we had never judged in the first place, there would be nothing to forgive. In other words, we didn't keep our focus on the divinity of that person. Instead, we decided the person did something that offended us and therefore required our forgiveness.

Unforgiveness—resentment, hate, and anger—

is probably at the root of most of the problems in our lives. But if we can just acknowledge that God is in each person, we'll see there's nothing to forgive, and . . . *voila* . . . the blocks to our own happiness are removed, sometimes instantaneously, as if incinerated. At times like these, no traces of our former ugly feelings can ever be found!

Forgive and Forget

If we say we'll forgive someone but won't forget what was done, we are not recognizing God in the person. Or if we say we'll forgive even if he or she was wrong, we are still not seeing God in the person. It all boils down to this: *There's nothing to forgive if you don't condemn in the first place, because you see the person as part of God.*

But there is *someone* to forgive, and this is yourself! Yes, if you've judged someone harshly, it is *you* who must be forgiven! "Forgive *me* for having judged you as unworthy of my love."

If there is someone in your life who you feel has wronged you, try to realize that since he or she is part of God, there is nothing to criticize and nothing to forgive. If anything, you need to ask this person's forgiveness of you.

We can ask forgiveness of others in two ways. Either we can go to that person directly and ask for forgiveness, or we can mentally ask the person during our meditation periods. Both ways work. In meditation we can even apologize to people who are deceased.

"Forgive *me*." That is the only forgiving that needs to be done. Try it. It will work miracles—guaranteed.

Once Over Lightly–

- Unforgiveness is probably at the root of most of the problems in our lives.
- If you feel you have to forgive, it means you judged someone harshly.
- When you acknowledge that God is in each person, you'll see there's nothing to forgive.
- There is nothing to forgive if you don't condemn in the first place because you see the person as part of God.
- "Forgive me" is the only forgiving that needs to be done.

The Wheels

"Always forgive your enemies—nothing annoys them so much."

—Oscar Wilde

Not forgiving may be the most difficult habit to break, but forgiving is essential for anyone on the spiritual path. When we perceive people as having harmed us or a loved one, physically or mentally or financially or however, we almost automatically resent them. Our attitude toward them changes: "How could I possibly love her after what she did to me?" But in withholding our love from them, we withhold it from ourselves, because love is not a static savings account waiting for us to withdraw and dole out to those who please us. Love is dynamic. Like a powerful river that can't be dammed up, it's a constant gushing of God's most special gift. We can't hoard it. We get the benefits of love *only* when we pass it on. Like a turbine that gets its power only when water rushes through it, we experience love only when we let love course through us.

Isometric Forgiveness

But forgiveness can almost seem impossible at times. Sometimes our hurts are so deep that we feel we're just not ready to forgive the person. If you can't forgive someone, try this: At least *want* to forgive. You may not be strong enough to forgive him or her now, but if you truly desire to do it, the strength will be there, sometimes without your even trying. It's like isometric exercises. Isometric exercises are workouts in which we try to move an immovable object. Just the striving to move the immovable object increases our strength. Then why not isometric forgiveness? The more you strive—even if you feel you're not getting anywhere with forgiveness—the more quickly you'll gain strength. Soon you will have enough strength to let go of the hurt and let feelings of love take its place. Do you see the paradox here? You can work on forgiving and build the strength. But when the strength is present, you *let go of the striving* to forgive and the inevitable tide of Spirit sweeps through you to clear away all hurt.

Ponder Point

Consider an eclipse of the sun. If you were to view it from outer space, you would see a round, black shadow moving slowly along the surface of Earth. But what if the moon suddenly stopped and the black shadow on our planet stayed in the same place? Obviously, without sunlight plants would die, and eventually that shadowed area would become devoid of all life.

Think of unforgiveness in the same way. If you hold onto unforgiveness, your soul will have a black, lifeless shadow as long as you allow that unforgiveness to linger there.

Warm-Ups

The need for forgiveness can only follow a harsh judgment. If we have never judged someone harshly in the first place, we have no reason to forgive him or her. Real forgiveness, therefore, is actually never judging in the first place!

Do you need to forgive someone—even a little bit? If so, what can you do to start the process? More important, what can you do so that it doesn't happen again?

Going for It

George Roemisch said, "Forgiveness is a God who will not leave us after all we've done." This, of course, implies that God will have judged us in the first place. You've probably heard someone say, or perhaps you've said it yourself, "God forgive him" or "God forgive me." *What are your thoughts about this phrase?*

Chapter 20

Being Grateful

The Wisdom

FREE OFFER –
No strings attached.

Would you believe God has made available to you free of charge everything you need to live a joy-filled life? Everything! It's because God's very nature is to give.

If we look around, we see so many marvelous and beautiful things that are evidence of God's giving. And how about all the wonderful things we cannot see, like love and wisdom and imagination? We get so used to all of God's gifts that we can forget to be thankful for them. We can take them for granted.

But this is a mistake, because it's only when we express our sincere thanks for something that we're able to have its full benefit.

When George Reedy was press secretary for President Lyndon Johnson, he was sent to the hospital for an ultrastrict diet to help him reduce. He was to eat *only* the food the hospital served him—nothing else was allowed. To help cheer him up, Reedy's office staff sent him a huge basket of flowers. Reedy responded, "Thanks for the flowers. They were delicious."

Whether expressed as joking around or as absolute sincerity, a "gratitude attitude" opens the door to more joy, more soul-satisfaction, in our lives. At the same time it gives a lift to others. We all like feeling appreciated.

Thankfulness Increases Our Blessings

Whatever we are thankful for increases and becomes even more useful to us. If you've ever trained a puppy to do tricks or to be obedient, you know it performed best when you praised it and showed your gratitude. All of life responds to the power of praise and thanksgiving.

We give thanks for our nourishing food, and it does its beneficial work in our bodies. We give thanks for our money, because we know our gratitude will help it to increase. We can praise and thank our families and friends, and our relationships will become even better. And who hasn't heard that plants which are praised grow better than those not praised?

If you want to enjoy more blessings in your life, praise what you have. Be genuinely thankful for it. Look about you for all God has given you and then, in your own way, express your gratitude.

Once Over Lightly–

- God has made available everything you need to live a joy-filled life.
- Only when you express your sincere thanks for something are you able to have its full benefits.
- A "gratitude attitude" opens the door to more joy.
- Whatever you are thankful for increases.

The Wheels

"If you can't be grateful for what you receive, be grateful for what you escape."

—Unknown

Words of thanksgiving, aloud or silent, draw additional blessings beyond those for which you are already thankful. How does this work? The more sincerely you give thanks for something, the more fully you have recognized its blessing. Recognizing you have received a blessing makes you even more open to receiving further blessings. But this openness shrinks unless we keep reminding ourselves that God's blessings flow nonstop. Speaking words of thanksgiving is a constant reminder of this fact and keeps us open to the flow.

Ponder Point

From military schools to Buddhist monasteries, when punishment is doled out, the one receiving the punishment *thanks* the one giving the punishment.

Warm-Ups

Here's an interesting exercise (you probably saw it coming!): *Including not only the things you have, but also (as the quote at the top suggests) the things you escaped, make a list of everything in your life for which you are thankful.*

Here's a not-so-obvious exercise: *Again, including not only the things you have, but also the things you escaped, make a list of all the things in your life for which you were* not *thankful when they happened but for which you are very thankful now.*

Going for It

[No fair skipping over this one, just because it sounds absurd. It isn't.]

Every time you have to do something you find distasteful, give thanks for it. Oh, come on . . . It's not that bad. For example, every time you pay a bill, give thanks (after all, you *did* receive some value or you would not be paying for it). How about when you have to listen to your parents or boss yelling at you? Give thanks for this because, whether they are justified or not in treating you this way, you are no doubt learning a lesson from it. (See "Ponder Point.")

People in recovery from alcohol and other drugs are constantly giving thanks. "Thank God I'm an alcoholic," they will say, because they realize it was the addiction that led them—even forced them—to seek a more spiritual life, to seek God.

So begin giving thanks, even when you feel it's the last thing you want to do.

Chapter 21

I Am Prosperous

The Wisdom

It's all a matter of shaping the clay.

While a close friend of ours was giving a tennis lesson, someone broke into his locker and stole his new $200 racquet. He was furious! For a full week he was in a rage over how this was so unjust, how he didn't deserve this, and how he had loved that new racquet so much. Finally, his wife calmed him down enough to explain how his behavior was actually hurting him. How could he be open to his prosperity, if all he did was complain about his loss? He got the message and decided then and there to change his attitude completely. He started seeing the theft as "just one of those things" and realized he had a right to God's blessings, no matter where they came from.

A few days after his attitude overhaul, he was talking to a fellow tennis teacher, who suggested he contact some of the tennis equipment companies, tell them he was a teacher who would like to use their equipment, and ask if they would be interested in sending him some. One company did reply, and offered him free equipment if he would use the company's brand exclusively and display it prominently. Our friend agreed and received the following top-of-the-line equipment: two racquets, three warm-up suits, three T-shirts, three hats, and three pairs each of tennis shorts, shoes, and socks!

Do you know people who are always worried about money, always complaining they never have enough? Know what? As long as they believe it, they never will!

When people are concerned about their money, it's because they aren't aware that God is the ultimate source of their supply. If we can latch onto the fact that God has given us everything we need in order to be happy, our worrying days will be over and we'll be able to accept more of God's riches. Actually, it's probably more accurate to say God has "made available" all we need, rather than God has "given" it to us. Why? Because we have our own parts to play, and it begins with *practicing the presence of God*—practicing feeling God's presence all around us at all times. With that mind-set, we'll develop the habit of allowing God's will to work out through us and we'll think and do things that express our divine nature.

Not only that, we'll catch ourselves continually trying to be better people, always loving and helpful to those around us. Living life this way brings us the riches of God, and whatever we need will come to us through ideas and opportunities. If we need money, we will *have* money. If we need wisdom, we will *have* wisdom. If we need love, we will *have* love. Whatever we need will tend to come into our lives when we function as God-aware. Sorry if this sounds overly simplistic or Pollyannaish. It's just the way it works.

Molding the Clay

It's said there is unformed "substance" everywhere, waiting to be shaped into whatever "molds" we provide.

If you have some modeling clay and want to form it into something, you press it into a mold. Whatever shape your mold is, that's the shape the clay will take on. The original clay is formless—of no definite shape. It has to be put into the mold so it can become *something.* With us, it's our deeply held thoughts and feelings that provide the mold for God's substance.

When we use the tools of our thoughts and

words—the mold for the "clay"—we don't necessarily have to understand the whole process, but we do have to have faith in it and trust that our blessings will come. Never doubt that you are rich with all of God's wealth. God wants you to make use of everything you need.

You understand, of course, that this is not the way most of the world thinks—or operates. It's easy to go along with the crowd and get caught up in useless beliefs. Sometimes it can seem a lot easier than having the courage to step out of the crowd and live these spiritual principles. This is a choice you'll have to make for yourself. In the long run, the rewards are far richer when you dare to do your own thinking and follow the guidance of your heart. It can be fun to run with the pack, but no pack ever became a hero or a leader or was remembered in history books. Sooner or later we all end up on the spiritual-evolution trail. It's you who will decide when the time is right for *you*. In the meantime, your prosperity is patiently waiting in the wings to make its grand entrance; it's listening for your cue.

Once Over Lightly–

- When you are concerned about money, you've forgotten that God is the ultimate source of your supply.

- Practicing the presence of God allows God's will to work through you.
- There is unformed "substance" waiting to be shaped by your thoughts and words.
- Never doubt you are rich with all of God's wealth. God wants you to use everything you need.

The Wheels

"Whoever said money can't buy happiness didn't know where to shop."

—Unknown

He was put up for adoption a few days after birth so he never knew his father. Yet, by the time his father died, the young man was rich. Trouble was, he had no way of knowing that his father, an eccentric wildcat driller, had made a large fortune in the oil business. Nor did the young man know that his father had died or that his father had left him his entire estate. When the lawyers finally located the young man, he was in a low-paying job with little prospect for a prosperous future. For just about his entire life, the young man had not known that he had a rich father and that he himself was rich beyond his dreams.

Our awareness or lack of awareness of God's blessings does not change the fact that these blessings exist. We are prosperous! Why would the creator create, if not to bestow upon the created all of Its love and blessings?

You can't do anything to earn God's blessings. They just *are*. They exist for you and await your awareness and then your pronouncement that you are claiming them . . . right now, right where you are, right in the middle of any circumstance you may be experiencing.

Ponder Point

John D. Rockefeller, one of the richest men who ever lived, stated, "I believe that the power to make money is a gift from God." *Do you agree or disagree with this statement? Why? Give your thoughts about his use of the following terms:*

power

make money

gift

Warm-Ups

We tend to think of prosperity as money. Yet there are people with billions of dollars whose main ambition is to keep on acquiring more. They couldn't spend their money on themselves in many lifetimes, and yet the thrust of their entire lives is to get even more. It's as if whoever dies with the most dollars wins. (Just to give you an idea of how much one billion dollars is, if you were to spend $10,000 every single day, you'd be broke in about 274 years. Of course, if you were getting even 4% interest, you could spend over $100,000 each day and *never* run out of money!)

Without being judgmental about their motives, do you feel these people are truly "rich"? Explain.

Going for It

Notwithstanding the quote to begin this section, can money buy happiness? What would it take for you to feel really prosperous? Would it be money? How about possessions? What about relationships? What that you love right now would you trade for money? Would you trade your self-respect? Would you trade the love of someone? What would you trade, and how much money would you want for it?

Chapter 22

Love Holds the World Together

The Wisdom

Turn up the candle-power
and aim in all directions.

Minnie was starved for affection. Throughout the many years she and Homer had been married, he'd never shown her any outward signs that he loved her. One day Minnie couldn't stand it any longer and blurted out, "Homer, why don't you ever tell me you love me?"

Homer replied without a smile: "Minnie, when we were married, I told you I loved you. If I ever change my mind, I'll let you know."

Homer may have thought that was good enough—that love never needs to be shared. But he was wrong. Love is the greatest power in the world, but it requires continual circulation to stay strong and vital. It was designed to be expressed.

If we open ourselves to love, we see that it certainly has to be the strongest attracting power in creation. It binds us all together in one great and marvelous union—all part of the one God. God *is* love. This love pulls each of us toward our true Christ Selves, making us more and more aware of our divinity. In the long run, love is stronger than hatred and wars—the personal battles as well as international ones.

It is God's love expressing itself through various natural laws that holds the planets in their orbits and us in our forms as human beings. Love is everywhere.

Love at All Times

But sometimes we humans attach strings to our love—we love only at certain times and we love only certain people. Maybe we feel we can love only the people who we feel love us or who are the same as we are. But this is not using our wonderful power of love in the correct way. The fact is that everyone *is* like us because, as we've said throughout this book, we are all part of the one God. The God in you is the same God in every other person, no matter how it may seem.

If we intend to live the way God designed us to, we have to start loving *everyone*. To love less than this is—are you ready?—not to love God. Our attention has to stay focused on the Christ nature of each person and not on outer appearances. We're not all cut from the same cookie cutter, so there will always be superficial differences. But we *are* all from the same batch of dough.

When we let the warmth of our love flow out from us in a complete circle, we touch everyone with it, and the entire world—especially our own immediate world—becomes a better place. We meet all people Christ-to-Christ, and our love automatically falls across their paths. To love in God's way is to let it flow freely, not withholding it from anyone. This is the ideal and, as with most of these universal principles, we may not be there yet. But when we realize that everyone wants to love and be loved and that everything people do is their way of crying out for that love, we begin to feel our own love moving in their direction. No kidding, it obviously takes a lot of practice to love everybody, but this is the way God loves *us*, and it's the way *we're* supposed to operate too. And here's a super bonus: *When you're loving, people can't help noticing your radiance and will love you in return.*

Love is a mighty magnet. Whatever we love, we attract into our lives. If we love God, we will attract blessings. Eventually each of us will realize that he or she is part of everyone else, and our love will touch everyone, because we are all one.

Once Over Lightly–

- Love requires continual circulation. It was designed to be expressed.
- Love is the strongest attracting power in the universe.
- To love in God's way is to let love flow freely, not withholding it from anyone.
- Whatever you love, you attract. When you love God, you attract God's blessings.
- God is love.

The Wheels

The teeth are smiling, but is the heart?

—Congolese proverb

Why is it that we tend to love only those who love us? If we really knew what love was all about, we would never allow another person to control the flow of love in us. Too often we treat love like a commodity to be hoarded and doled out to only certain people. The Truth is that love flows from God not *to* us but *through* us. So when we withhold love from someone, we are withholding it from ourselves. Yipes—how dumb! It's like tearing out the beautiful flower bed on your front lawn because you've had an argument with your neighbor and don't want her to enjoy it. What we do to another, we do to ourselves.

What would you think of a songwriter who decides not to write anymore songs because his enemies would enjoy them too? Or an inventor who stopped inventing because she only wanted the people she loved, not those she didn't love, to enjoy the fruits of her labor? These might sound like ridiculous analogies, but withholding love is like that.

Ponder Point

All the love that is available to us or will ever be available to us is available right now. We are filled to capacity with love at all times, and can't possibly love more than we are capable of right now. We may not choose to share this love, but that, of course, is up to us. No one can make us love more than we ourselves decide to.

That's because love is intrinsic—it is in us already. It doesn't need to be manufactured, only expressed. Watch an abused child hug a teddy bear, and you will see love fill the child. But tear the teddy bear open, and you won't find an ounce of love in it. Where did the love the child felt come from? Not from the bear, but from within the child herself. The teddy bear merely served as a catalyst to allow the child to express the love she already had inside of her.

Other people don't dictate if or when we love—*we do*. To love or not to love is always our decision.

Warm-Ups

We are continually sending out emotional energy. It could be a love-filled energy, a hate-filled energy or something in-between. Mother Teresa described the conscious choice she made about her energy with these words: "Why should I expend energy in anger that I can expend in love?"

Have you made a conscious choice yet? Are you holding your love back in places? The object is to let it beam out in a complete circle like a candle or a bright light, falling on everyone and everything in its path. It doesn't matter where you begin. You can jump-start the process with friends and family members. As you feel love for these special people, see them as the filament of a lightbulb—a "love" bulb, in this case—and as you direct your love to them, see that filament lighting up everything and everyone around them, eventually lighting the world with love.

Going for It

Think of the one person in your life whom you love the most. Feel the love that fills you when you think of him or her. It's a warm and wonderful feeling, right? Well, this is the feeling you're supposed to have for *all* people. You need to love the person who took something from you as much as you love your dearest friend. (Hey, nobody said it was easy, but that doesn't change the fact that it's something we all must eventually do.)

Chapter 23

What Is This Thing Called Faith?

The Wisdom

Your faith is unlimited.
Invest it wisely.

Maybe the simplest definition is this: Faith is expectation.

Let's say you've learned how to ride a bicycle. Now you never have to stop and think about it or analyze it. You just expect that you can ride a bike, so you do. You have faith in your ability to ride a bicycle.

Let's take this up a notch to faith in God. Because we are part of the great presence of God, we have every right to *expect* (have faith) that our lives will be blessed. If we really believe this is true, we'll expect it and we'll *act* as if it were true.

An interesting phenomenon occurs, however, when we gain spiritual maturity. The landscape of our faith changes. Instead of expecting *specific* results to happen in our lives, our faith becomes more invested in God's overall design for the universe. At that point we simply know beyond all discussion that God works out the best plan for each of us. The path will eventually lead us to this more general, unquestioned faith.

No More Faith Needed

Although we may gain a *recognition* of more faith, in reality we don't "gain" faith. We can discover faith. We can redirect faith. We can become more aware of faith. We can even deepen faith. But we can't *gain* faith. Why? Because, like love, we already have all the capacity for faith we will ever need. So the issue is never really how much faith we have, but how we have invested the faith we already have.

But in the meantime, there's nothing wrong with faith in specifics. The problem is that faith can only reach to the self-imposed boundaries of our present consciousness. That means it is we who limit our faith by putting boundaries on it. For instance, if we say we inherit wholeness from God (which we do) and then go around complaining about aches and pains or go around smoking or doing drugs or eating junk foods or being a couch potato, where's the real faith? Is it the wholeness we are voicing or is it our unwholesome actions that reflect our present consciousness? Our actions are a gauge of the strength and direction of our faith, and they are always revealing where our true faith lies. They invariably show us what we're *really* expecting. Check it out.

Once Over Lightly–

- Faith is expectation.
- With mature faith, you know to trust God's plan for you.
- You have all the faith you'll ever need. The question is, How have you invested it?
- Your actions are a gauge of the strength and direction of your faith.

The Wheels

"It is by believing in roses that one brings them to bloom."

—French proverb

A friend of ours from Missouri told us this story. In the early days of the United States, when many people journeyed on foot, a weary traveler came upon the Missouri River. There was no bridge in those days, and since it was winter, the mighty river was covered with ice. Night was approaching, and it was urgent that he reach the other side. But would the ice hold his weight? Torn by the need to get across and the fear that the ice would break, he finally decided to creep slowly on his hands and knees; he hoped this would distribute his weight as much as possible. It was slow, painful going. His heart pounded and his limbs trembled.

When he was about halfway across, the traveler heard the sound of whistling in the twilight behind him. There came a man vigorously driving a horse-drawn wagon of lumber across the ice to the other side. And here was the traveler on his hands and knees, quaking because he feared that that same ice might not support him.

Some of us find ourselves creeping through life, not trusting the power and promise of God, while others sail merrily along, expecting life to be supportive—always trusting that things will work out right.

Ponder Point

True faith begins with faith in God. Don't be misled into thinking you only have to believe in something for it to come into your life. That's not what faith is all about. Faith begins with centering on God within you. If you sincerely long to experience the presence of God, if you are centered in God, then you can have complete faith that your life will be lifted to a new level. Why? Because when you trust the presence of God living *as* you, God will fill you with divine ideas. And it is these divine ideas that contain the seed of your blessing.

Warm-Ups

This feels like the right time to take an inventory of just exactly where your faith is. Is your faith in poor health or failing grades or dead-end jobs or unhappy relationships? Are any of these what you have now? Is this what you're expecting more of in the future? Check to see what the circumstances of your life are telling you about your faith.

Give some serious thought to what steps you can take to increase your faith in God's blessings. (Remember, faith begins with the awareness of God's presence in your life.)

Going for It

Many religions have complete faith in their own version of what will happen in the future. Some religions taught that the world would end at the year 1000; others, that it would end at the year 2000. Some teach that Jesus will return; others, that Jesus never existed. Some have complete faith in their founder, while others think the "saint" is a charlatan. *How do you reconcile many religious organizations' faith that theirs is the only true religion?*

Chapter 24

Why Am I Here?

The Wisdom

You're a piece in the cosmic jigsaw puzzle.

It just might be that the best way God can be known to the world is through us—through the human race.

We are each an indispensable part of God's plan for the world. We each express God in our own individual ways, so only we can play our own particular roles.

Ever put together a jigsaw puzzle? If you have, you know there's a mound of pieces, each unique. The picture is not complete until you have put the last piece in place. In the same way, each person is a piece of God's universe. Each of us is different from the others, but it takes everyone, being authentic to his or her true Self, to make the plan complete. A drum would never try to sound like a flute, nor would a violin try to be a tuba. Only when each instrument in an orchestra authentically expresses its true self is beautiful music possible. (Since we are all such unique expressions of God, all necessary to God's plan, we can only imagine what beautiful music God must envision for us!)

The purpose of our existence is to be part of God's evolution of the divine plan for the universe. Our first step, then, is to be aware that we're essential to the plan. Next, we can keep a close watch on the thoughts that come leaping into our minds. Are they worthwhile thoughts? Will they bring blessings? If a negative, not-so-hot thought pops up, do we throw it out right away and replace it with a better one? Let's face it; negative thoughts do pop up—it happens. But the trick is to junk them at once, before they do any harm.

What about our words—are they authentically spoken from the heart, from our spiritual awareness? If so, they have power to bring tremendous blessings. Let's make our words the kindest and most loving and helpful that we can.

The last thing we can check is our actions. What kind of things are we doing? Are we being authentic to our divine design by expressing our divine nature? Or are we settling for less?

These are all significant ways we can be more of

our real Selves. And being our real Selves, after all, is why we're here. Being authentic is our way of co-operating with God's design for the universe. And responding with kindness and compassion in every situation is the perfect gauge of our authenticity.

Once Over Lightly–

- You are an indispensable part of God's plan for the world.
- The purpose of your existence is to be part of God's evolution of the divine plan for the universe.
- You can express your real purpose only when you are authentic.
- The extent to which you respond with kindness is the perfect gauge of your authenticity.

The Wheels

"There are no precedents: You are the first You that ever was."

—Christopher Morley

Why are you here? To be authentic. Nothing more, nothing less. But in that statement lies a lifetime of commitment.

Since the Creator can only know Itself through Its creations, it's obvious you were created to be a unique expression of God. When you are authentically yourself, you are expressing one facet of God most accurately. A diamond is valuable simply because each facet receives light and reflects it in a direction unique to itself. If every facet of a diamond decided to reflect light just like every other facet, it would be a rather dull piece of rock.

Ponder Point

Why is it so difficult to act in a way that is an authentic expression of what God created, of who we are? Is it peer pressure? Is it a feeling that we are not quite good enough? But such attitudes imply that God made a mistake with us and that we need to conform more with what society expects of us. Doesn't make a whole lot of sense, does it?

Warm-Ups

Name the people with whom you are most authentic and explain why it is easy to be more authentic with them.

Name the people with whom you are least authentic. Describe why it is difficult to be authentic with them. (The best way to do this exercise is to catch yourself when you are not being authentic.)

Going for It

Probably the worst thing we can say about someone is, "What a phoney!" We all want to feel we are straightshooters, genuine "what you see is what you get" people, who have no need to try to be something we're not.

Make a list of the ten people you know who seem to be the most authentic.

Now make a list of ten people you know whom you admire the most.

Compare the list. Are there many duplicates?

New Beginnings

The Wisdom

Look inside yourself
and follow your heart.

This entire book has presented you with ideas and concepts about God, the universe, and how you fit in. The pages are filled with words trying to convey teachings and principles about recognizing God's presence and how to express your own divine nature. Yet after all is said and done, it's not concepts and principles themselves that matter. *How we live our lives is where it's at.*

When you have reached the point where most of the time you know you are one with God, your entire self will have changed. Much of the negative stuff that was in your life will have disappeared. Your mind will be different.

There's only one person in the entire universe

who can keep you from attaining this—from being authentically you—and that's *you*! You can open the door to God's blessings, or you can pull down the shades and hide from them. It's your choice. Do you pick the negative—anger, resentment, hatred, complaining, time-wasting—or do you choose the positive, the beautiful, the compassionate, the loving?

We have choices to make many times every day. What we choose determines what our lives will be like. God is waiting to be recognized and has been right here all the time. Look inside yourself and follow your heart, and you'll automatically be following God's plan for you. If you want it to, today can be the first day of your *new* life. It can be a real birthday for you—a whole new beginning! The best is still to come.

And that is the simple truth.

The Wheels

"One doesn't discover new lands without consenting to lose sight of the shore for a very long time."

—André Gide

New lands await us now—spiritual frontiers beckon. All the days and all the years ahead are uncharted territory, as yet unlived by any human being. They are ours to breathe life into and make of them what we will.

The time and effort you've invested in these 25 chapters should serve you well in making the most of every moment of your life. Let your reaction to each of the following statements serve as a bellwether to help evaluate your progress. Or if some time in the future you are going through a particularly difficult period of your life, you can use them to get yourself back on track.

I find myself smiling more.

I am a harmonizer.

I remember the divinity of each person.

My first response is kindness.

I am an understanding person.

I let people live their own lives.
I cooperate with God's laws for the physical body.
I discover the blessings in situations.
If I have feelings of hurt or anger, I let go of them quickly.
I am a grateful person.
I have faith that God knows best.
I devote time regularly to sitting still and being aware of God as my life.

Keep in mind that, since the soul evolves, your reactions to these statements will evolve as well. Don't be hard on yourself if you're disappointed with some of your reactions. Give your life the light touch—see the humor in things, and you'll be happier as well as easier for others to be with. Also, remember that everyone in the world wants to be loved as much as you do.

So be good to yourself. Be sure to drink plenty of water, floss your teeth every night, and always wear your sunscreen.

And, finally, let's face it—since most of the gain in our lives comes by simply grinding it out rather than by making spectacular leaps, we'll leave you with these words of wisdom from Woody Allen—"Eighty percent of success is showing up."

About the Authors

Mary-Alice and Richard Jafolla are the authors of the popular *The Quest* and *Adventures on the Quest*, currently published in three languages. Former directors of Silent Unity, the husband-and-wife team has long been in demand as speakers in the United States and abroad.

In addition to numerous Unity books, audiocassettes, and articles, including *Nourishing the Life Force, Quest 2000, The Quest for Prayer,* and *Beside Still Waters*, Mary-Alice and Richard have authored many other works for national publications.

The Jafollas reside in Vero Beach, Florida, with their adopted greyhound, Sunny.

Printed in the U.S.A. B0110